TREKKERS

TRUE STORIES BY FANS FOR FANS

TREKKERS

TRUE STORIES BY FANS FOR FANS

Edited by Nikki Stafford

ECW PRESS

Published by ECW PRESS
2120 Queen Street East, Suite 200, Toronto, Ontario, Canada M4E 1E2

NATIONAL LIBRARY OF CANADA CATALOGUING IN PUBLICATION DATA

Main entry under title:
Trekkers: stories by fans for fans

ISBN 1-55022-503-0

1. Star Trek televison programs —Anecdotes. 2. Science fiction fans — Anecdotes. I. Stafford, Nikki, 1973–

PN1992.8.S74T74 2002 791.45'75 C2001-904085-7

Cover and Text Design: Tania Craan
Typesetting: Gail Nina
Production: Mary Bowness
Printing: AGMV MARQUIS
Front cover artwork: Antonio M. Rosario / Getty Images / The Image Bank

This book is set in Minion and Univers

The publication of *Trekkers* has been generously supported by the Canada Council, the Ontario Arts Council, and the Government of Canada through the Book Publishing Industry Development Program. Canadä

DISTRIBUTION

CANADA: General Distribution Services, 325 Humber College Blvd., Toronto, ON M9W 7C3

UNITED STATES: Independent Publishers Group, 814 North Franklin Street, Chicago, Illinois 60610

EUROPE: Turnaround Publisher Services, Unit 3, Olympia Trading Estate, Coburg Road, Wood Green, London N2Z 6T2

AUSTRALIA AND NEW ZEALAND: Wakefield Press, 17 Rundle Street (Box 2066), Kent Town, South Australia 5071

PRINTED AND BOUND IN CANADA

ECW PRESS
ecwpress.com

Table of Contents

Introduction

About a year ago I was watching the documentary *Trekkies*, and was fascinated by some of the people on the show (not to mention recognizing them as being very similar to several friends of mine) and I thought to myself that there must be hundreds of other stories like the ones in the film. The *Star Trek* franchise has been around since 1966, and has spawned generations of Trekkies and Trekkers, and with its message of equality, peace, and goodwill to others, has changed how we watch television and how we view life. I put out a notice in early 2001 asking for stories, and at first they just trickled in. With some help from the wonderful Benjamin Winn, who runs the *Star Trek Newsletter* (www.treknewsletter.com), I was eventually able to get dozens of replies from people around the world. I was amazed, amused, and touched by the heartfelt and powerful stories I received from so many people.

Trekkers/Trekkies are people who are laughed at, mocked, and the butt of so many jokes — and have been for years — but that's only because they are misunderstood. They don't believe the show and characters are real, they don't speak only using lines from *Star Trek*, and they don't know every Klingon word in existence (well, most of them don't). They're caring, kind, charitable people who live by the credo of the show. And considering the show advances notions that some day, the world could be a place where all races, colors, religions, and species could live together in harmony, well, what's wrong with hoping for that?

Since September 2001, the world has been focusing on issues of freedom, peace, and tolerance of other people. Interestingly, I received as many submissions from Trekkers before September 11th as I did afterwards. And the wording was exactly the same before as it was after. While the rest of the world was awakened to the possibilities of cooperation and working together to achieve common goals, Trekkers were way ahead of them. Gene Roddenberry had a vision so many years ago, and he has legions of fans who share that vision.

I would like to thank everyone who submitted stories, photographs, and artwork. I wish I could have used every story that was sent to me. Thanks also to the administrators of the *Trek* news sites who helped spread the word when I was looking for stories, and especially to Benjamin Winn for sending out notice after notice to his readers, and for sending out press releases to the sites. This book truly couldn't have been done without you. And finally, many people have asked me why I chose to refer to *Star Trek* fans as "Trekkers" in the title rather than "Trekkies," and the answer is simple: I received many letters and e-mails from fans begging me not to use the perceived derogatory term, "Trekkies," when referring to *Trek* fans, even though many fans are quite proud of the term. I received no complaints about the use of "Trekkers," so I went with that one. However, you'll find throughout the book both terms are used.

These stories represent a tiny slice of the fandom, but are powerful and moving stories of what we can do when we all work together, and how a small, seemingly insignificant television show has risen up to become one of the most influential pop culture icons of the 20th and 21st centuries. The fans have become as legendary as the show, and for good reason. The stories in this book have been written for other Trekkers to read. Stories of triumph over adversity, meeting friends through a mutual adoration of *Star Trek*, and starting up Web sites to promote the show. Stories of meeting the celebrities who appeared on the show, sneaking onto the sets of *Voyager*, and learning to mourn the loss of someone through *Star Trek*. I hope you enjoy them as much as I have.

NIKKI STAFFORD
nikki_stafford@yahoo.com
FEBRUARY 2002

Star Trek Changed My Life

Star Trek is part of a very small group of shows that has had a far-reaching effect on the lives of its viewers. I received so many personal stories from fans about how the show changed their lives, and many of them were very touching: a boy with cerebral palsy watches *Star Trek* at a young age and finds the strength within himself to overcome his condition; a young girl watches "Vina" weave a sensuous spell over the captain and vows to become a bellydancer; a soldier in Vietnam discovers the show just before he's shipped off to fight; and a man takes the lessons he learned from *Star Trek* as a kid and applies them to a school where he eventually becomes principal. *Star Trek* has given many people the strength to go on after hardships because of its message of hope, equality, and peace.

I chose to begin the section with Jason Lighthall's piece, because so many Trekkers and Trekkies have been ridiculed for no reason other than the show that they watch, and I thought this was a very mature and well written story about why it's okay to be a Trekkie.

I'm Proud to Be a Star Trek Fan

BY JASON LIGHTHALL

Why is it that people regard *Star Trek* fans differently than they do people who don't watch the show? I'm a *Star Trek* fan, and I'm proud to say so. Am I so different that I should be treated differently? There are a lot of things to be proud of, as well as some problems that go with being a *Star Trek* fan.

One of the most common stereotypes of a *Star Trek* fan is that they're geeks, and because of this misconception we are sometimes mistreated. We are thought of as weird outsiders in the normal world. Being a part of this community has been very hard for me, especially when I was younger, simply because I've had to deal with the ongoing torment that is associated with being a *Star Trek* fan. Though, I'm proud to say that I found a way to deal with these problems.

Throughout my early years of being a high school student I concealed the fact that I was a fan of the show. I was afraid people would make fun of me, and I would be unable to achieve the goal that most immature high school students wanted: popularity or the need to fit in. When I approached my junior and senior years of high school, I approached them with a different attitude. Over the years of watching *Star Trek* I began to realize that people are different and unique, and because of this I grew more self-confident with each passing year.

I became more daring in the fact that I literally showed everybody that I loved *Star Trek*. On Halloween, starting my junior year, I dressed up in a Starfleet uniform that I got from my parents. I wasn't afraid to show it off, but of course I had to deal with people smirking and sometimes laughing at me. That was tough to deal with, but I swallowed my pride and dealt with it. For my senior year, I did something that no other student in the history of my school had ever done: I dressed up in the Starfleet uniform and had my senior pictures taken with them, and I had one of the pictures with the uniform put into the yearbook. It was incredible: I had people coming up to me and asking me how I could do such a thing, and that I must have had a lot of guts to go through with it.

The reason that I grew more confident about myself was

William Shatner poses with four intergalactic fans. (Photo courtesy Marc B. Lee)

because I learned what kind of a community *Star Trek* fandom is. *Star Trek* fans are intelligent and sophisticated people who love to dream about what our future could be. *Star Trek* spans all generations and is something that unites people. One of the most common goals for *Star Trek* is to teach morals and values. The show has literally thousands of different species from different worlds who come together to try to better themselves as a civilization, while trying to deal with social conflicts in the right way.

There are a lot of benefits that come with being a part of the *Star Trek* community, such as long-lasting friendships. In grade school, I started hanging out with someone because we were both interested in *Star Trek*, and we're still friends to this day. In the *Star Trek* world, there are also social conflicts that take place just like in our real world. The people on the show are able to deal with these conflicts in a peaceful and diplomatic way. I've begun to learn new ways of dealing with people and respecting them in a more mature and social manner. Most people who are *Star Trek* fans are also highly motivated, and are more likely to succeed in life because of that. We want to change our future so that we can improve our life and the lives of others.

I look back now and I can see how being a part of the *Star Trek* community has changed me. It has changed me for the better, because I'm more confident when dealing with people and have learned better communication skills. And even though there are a few problems that I have had to deal with, I've learned to deal with those and to treat people with the utmost respect. So, I can say with great joy that I am proud to be a *Star Trek* fan.

Overcoming Obstacles

BY DOUGLAS W. MAYO

In 1968, the world I lived in got a bit bigger. It was a time of national conflict set in motion by the calls for change. As a nine-year-old boy, I too struggled, and began a personal journey for change that continues to this day.

In 1959, I was born prematurely with Cerebral Palsy (CP) affecting my entire right side. I was the second of eventually four boys, all close in age. Because of my CP, neither my parents nor my brothers knew how to interact with me in any meaningful way, nor did they try.

In part it was not their fault; my mother had to deal with the untimely accidental death of my father in 1962, just 10 weeks after giving birth to my youngest brother. She was suddenly single and jobless with four young children, one who needed more than she could give. Those were desperate times for her and for us.

As for my brothers, with all of us being close in age, competition was a natural occurrence. Through the years, all of my brothers excelled in the physical world around us; they ran, swam, and played, leaving me on the sideline to wish and hope for a body that could join them. In academics, I could not compete either, it was like I could not focus or express my thoughts on paper or to others. The teachers and the school system fell into the same trap as my parents and brothers did; they did not know how to reach me, so they did not try.

In 1965, my mother remarried. In 1966 I had a cord-lengthening procedure done to my right leg in the hopes that I would be able to walk without the use of the heavy brace I had been using up to that point. It was a long summer of being carried everywhere as I recovered. I had envisioned returning to school a new boy, able to run, play, and think like the other children. It was not to be: that school year passed along as many others did, with me on the sidelines — physically.

Mentally, my mind raced, searching for pathways that would finally make learning for me easier. In grade school, just learning the basics of reading, writing, and math were doubly troublesome for me, and I ended up in summer school every year just to get to the next grade.

In 1968, it was as if magic did exist. For the first time I began to understand what I was reading, to understand the sounds and meaning of the words. The next few years for me were truly awakening ones. I read all sorts of books, from biographies of Ben Franklin and Thomas Edison, to *Moby Dick*, to real-life stories of the FBI, to stories by Isaac Asimov. I spent my weekends reading at the public library.

At school, we were able to order paperback books through a wonderful program called Readers. One month the catalog came in and I spotted a *Star Trek* book. It was a collection of adaptations by James Blish of the episodes shown on TV, something of which I was vaguely aware. I ordered that book and could hardly contain myself for the month it took to arrive.

Here was a world through a story in a book that challenged humankind to rise above physical appearances, to work together as a team for a greater good, something I had wanted on a personal level all of my life. Within this book and the many others I eagerly purchased were stories about exploration of new worlds and ideas, of honor and true commitment, and of heroes and sacrifice.

In July of 1969, humankind did rise above the confusion of the times and landed a man on the moon. I, too, celebrated that moment on Costume Day at a summer day camp; I was photographed for the local newspapers in my makeshift astronaut suit made from brown paper bags. For the rest of that summer into the fall, kids across the nation were constructing their own lunar landers from paper being given out free by Texaco. I made a space fleet of those landers.

I remember building my very first model that summer, and it was of the Starship *Enterprise* from *Star Trek*. I flew that ship down the streets of my neighborhood to show-and-tell time in the classroom. At night I would keep the ship in a specially constructed "space-dock" (a shoebox), underneath my bed.

Through repeats I watched every episode of *Star Trek*. I understood *Star Trek*'s vision for humankind to take hold, a place where I would be accepted regardless of my disabilities, and I desperately wanted it in my own life. *Star Trek* for me became more than television, it became my hope of a better life.

Just when I thought I had worked past all the obstacles my CP threw at me, I was involved in a terrible car accident in 1978. After fracturing my lower spine, shattering my left kneecap and smashing my right ankle, along with other multiple injuries, I thought I'd traveled back in time to my childhood. My doctors once again were telling me that I was never going to walk again. The next few years were difficult and painful, but I would not, *could* not, let all I had achieved go down the drain for not trying. Like James T. Kirk, I did not accept defeat; I made it my mission in life to find alternatives, to survive.

As I grew older, I incorporated *Star Trek*'s hope and vision of what mankind can achieve as my own. I have subtly weaved *Star*

Trek's ideals into my personal life as well as prompting personal growth in others. When I worked with troubled teens as a residential counselor I often used *Star Trek* as an education tool to strive for something more, to accept what may appear to be different, and to take risks. When I worked with developmentally challenged individuals, I used the *Star Trek* universe to once again teach valuable lessons about communication and conflict resolution. I even brought one client to a *Star Trek* convention to show him all the different types of fans who love the show. I could tell from the light in his eyes and the smile on his face that that one afternoon would forever burn bright in his memory. On the way back to the group home he thanked me for teaching him about *Star Trek*'s life lessons, and for sharing the moment with him. Neither one of us will ever forget that moment.

When I rose to become the president of my local union I had the opportunity to put a number of *Star Trek* life lessons to use: how to be a good leader, make a tough decision, make a difference, look for other options. These are all valuable lessons and they can be found through a variety of sources, but for me *Star Trek* is where I looked for affirmation.

Star Trek, *Thy Name Is English Teacher!*

BY GEERT BONTE

I live in Belgium and I watched *Star Trek* (the original series) on Belgian television when I was still a kid. We could only receive a handful of television stations back then. A few years later, *Star Trek* wasn't on Belgian TV anymore, but we got cable TV and were able to watch the BBC.

Although my understanding of the English language was very limited, I started watching all those wonderful *Star Trek* episodes on BBC 2. I had already seen them all, but I just loved to watch them again. The fact that there were no Dutch subtitles this time and I didn't understand much of the dialogue didn't bother me at all.

In fact, my knowledge of English improved, just by watching *Star Trek*! Now I have a fairly good knowledge of English, despite the fact that I didn't learn much English at school, where more stress was put on French, Belgium's second official language (besides Dutch, my native language). I really believe that my English would be a lot worse if I hadn't been a *Star Trek* fan for so long.

Now I prefer watching movies and television shows without subtitles, and if there are subtitles, I don't read them any more. You would be surprised how much of the picture you lose by reading the subtitles. You're constantly watching the bottom part of the screen, and you barely see what's going on in the rest of the picture!

I enjoy reading *Star Trek* magazines and *Star Trek* novels (which are not available in Dutch), and I've even started reading Shakespeare (inspired by the many Shakespearean actors in *Trek*). So thank you, *Star Trek*, for teaching me English!

A Dream of a Better World

BY GREGORY NEWMAN

The year was 1966 and I was a black soldier in the U.S. Army. I was stationed at Fort Monmouth, N.J., training to become an

Electronic Technician. The Vietnam War was blazing and U.S. servicemen and -women were dying. I had to serve nearly three years in the army, and I knew that I would probably have to go to Vietnam. And there was a damn good chance I could get killed over there. I went home to Philly on leave and my sisters told me about this great science-fiction show called *Star Trek*. I missed the first broadcast but caught the second one and got hooked on *Star Trek* while in the service.

I continue to watch *Star Trek* to this day. It recognizes our world of war, racial prejudice, and poverty and gives us hope of a future glorious world, a world of benevolent human beings of all races who work together with beings from other worlds to peacefully explore the vast universe with awe, courage, hope, love, and curiosity. I will always be thankful to Gene Roddenberry, the 1966 *Star Trek* cast, and Paramount for creating *Star Trek*. In 1966 when I and other servicepeople in the armed forces were fighting and dying in Vietnam while prejudice, poverty, and drug wars raged around us, *Star Trek* kept alive a dream of a better world. And after the war, *Star Trek* kept Vietnam veterans focused on that possibility. I hope *Star Trek* can continue to help others think on life's positive side when there is trouble.

When I was collecting submissions I received a videotape in the mail from a bellydancer in New York named Shamira, and it was amazing. I emailed her to get her to talk about her experiences as a Trekkie, and she explained how it was Star Trek *that made her choose her profession.*

The Sensuous Influence of Star Trek

BY SHAMIRA

www.shamiradance.com

I began watching *Star Trek* at a young age, and little did I know then what an impact it would have on the rest of my life. The green Orion dancing girl who mesmerized Captain Pike in "The Cage" and "The Menagerie" also mesmerized an impressionable girl. I always knew I would grow up to be a professional dancer. At the time, I was studying ballet. To see this sensuous, exotic woman writhing around enticing a Starship captain somewhere in outer space while big-headed aliens watched . . . let's just say I never forgot it! Years later I began my career as a bellydancer. My dream had come true, I had become "Vina." (Er . . . except for the green part. And the happily-ever-after-with-a-handsome-starship-captain-living-on-another-planet part. But hey, it could happen!)

I believe *Star Trek* is a cosmic dance. It paints a romantic, exciting design in the universe, in human thought, in my mind. It directs my perceptions away from the mundane and points me toward grandeur and endless possibility. I am drawn to both *Star Trek* and bellydancing for the same reason — they are fascinating, glamorous, and mysterious.

I am now a bellydance instructor and performer, and teach sold-out courses in the New York City area. While it has been a lot of hard work, it has also given me the opportunity to meet an extraordinary variety of people. I have danced in Lincoln Center and Radio City Music Hall, and I have danced on a bowling alley and in a tire garage. All of my students know that I am a Trekkie, and they get a kick out of it.

(Photos courtesy Shamira)

I made a bellydance instructional video called *Bellydancing: The Sensuous Workout.* One of the cameramen was a fellow Trekkie, as was the graphic artist who designed the cover (he used the *Trek* font on the back cover of the video). The instructional/workout part of the video is in several sections, the last section is called "Shimmies." At the very end of that section, as it is fading to black, I do the Vulcan hand salute.

As a bonus on the video, I included a music video, a montage that fuses *Trek* and bellydancing. It starts out with me as a little girl (played by my goddaughter) watching *Star Trek* on TV. Little Shamira falls asleep in bed reading a book about bellydancing. As we enter her dreams, she has "beamed down" into a nightclub and she is a swirling bellydancer. Then all of a sudden she is grown up and dancing with Picard, Riker, Worf, and Seven of Nine — anything can happen in your dreams. And anything can happen in real life! This entire music video could not have existed without *Star Trek*.

The project originally came about through *Star Trek* newsgroups. I was a regular poster at a *ST* newsgroup, where I met and made friends with many fellow Trekkies. One of them was a musician/composer named "Wavemaker." We became very good friends, and I became a big fan of his music. He sent me one of the pieces he had written and asked me to suggest a title for it. I came up with "Harem Heat," and I immediately wanted to choreograph a dance routine to it. The final product is something I am very proud of. It also gives me a good laugh: the instructional video has done very well on amazon.com, which means that people from all over the world have ordered it. It goes along for 49 minutes teaching bellydancing, then out of the blue, here is this *Star Trek*/bellydancing video montage. So I like to picture non-*Trek* people and the bewildered looks on their faces when they get to that part.

Star Trek continues to infiltrate my life; it is just a part of who I am. I not only grew up studying dance, I also studied piano intensely, but ultimately chose a career in dance. About six months ago I dusted off my magnificent Steinway grand and started playing again. What did I play? The theme from "The Inner Light," a theme that every Trekkie is familiar with. I have since written four piano variations on this theme, one of which is a piano/guitar duet that I will play with Wavemaker. I will be going into a recording studio soon to make a CD. Right now the working title is *The Inner Light Variations: A Tribute to Captain Picard*. Stay tuned!

A Quest to Be Captain

BY MICHAEL ANTHONY LEE

My first recollection of *Star Trek* came on a Saturday morning. I was just a boy, looking forward to my weekly cartoon fix, when I walked into the living room and found my older brother controlling the television set. He was watching something called *Star Trek*, and would be doing so for the next hour. Now, I didn't know what this *Star Trek* was and I really didn't care. What I did know was that it was coming between me and my Saturday morning cartoons. My pleas to Mom going unanswered, I returned to my room with a sour look. This was my introduction into the world Gene Roddenberry had created, and I must admit, it left a bad taste in my mouth.

Years later, the hype for *Star Trek: The Next Generation* was everywhere. On the night of the series premiere, everyone was excited; everyone, that is, except me. Returning to the same living room, I saw a familiar sight. Not only did my brother control the television, but this time my mother was with him. Against my will, they talked me into giving this new show a chance.

"I don't know, it's still *Star Trek*," I said. But who could say no to Mom?

Watching this show, I was immediately confused. "Who's

the bald guy?" I asked. "That's not Captain Kirk." Although I had never watched the original series, I had still picked up a few things from accidental encounters, and this show just wasn't right. There was no Spock, no Kirk, and what was with this android guy? "This is stupid!" I said, and immediately left. Once again, *Star Trek* had sent me to my room in a foul state.

I enjoyed fantasy shows, stories of myth and legends, but all this space stuff was confusing and didn't interest me in the least. Having no idea why this show had become so popular, I concluded that the whole world had obviously gone mad.

A few years later, while in my room avoiding *Trek*, I decided to call my nephew to kill some time.

"Can't talk, I'm watching a show," he quickly informed me. "I'll call you back in an hour."

Hey, maybe I was missing out on something good here. "What're you watching?" I asked.

"*Star Trek*!" was his happy reply. The two words I never thought I would hear from someone with such good taste in television.

"You're a nerd!" I roared and slammed down the phone. But he was a persistent nerd. An hour later, he called me back and tried to explain that the show was really good. Now, not only did I question his sanity, but I also declared him a traitor to everything we believed in. "You're nuts," was all I could say, but he wouldn't give in so easily. He made me a bet, to put my prejudice aside and watch three episodes. After that, if I wanted to stop watching, I could. But, he suspected I wouldn't.

I'd like to go on record here and say that for the first time, and probably the last, Chris Lee was right about something. Not only did I continue watching the show, I learned to love it. I was like the

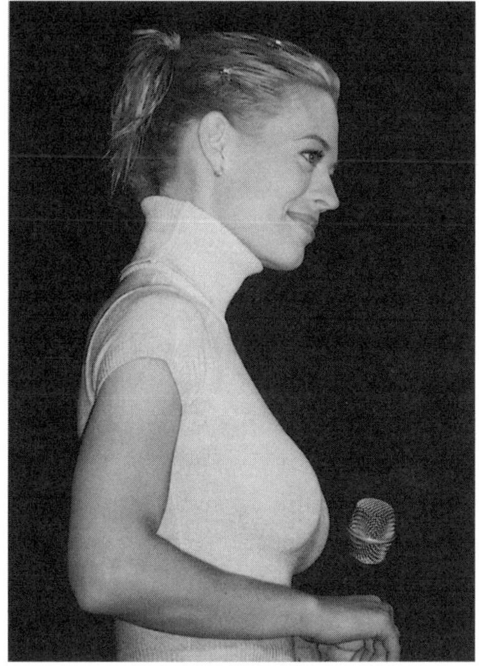

Jeri Ryan (Photo courtesy Marc B. Lee)

Grinch who finally discovered the true meaning of Christmas. And that android guy? He became my favorite character.

I sent Mr. Spiner a letter telling him so. He replied, and included an autographed photo that I eagerly hung on my wall.

Now, I don't remember hearing about Hell freezing over, or if there were two moons in the sky, but somewhere around my late teens or early twenties, I became a Trekker. Who would have guessed? Right around this time of miracles, when almost anything was possible, *Voyager* was making its grand debut. Of course this was another exciting evening at the house and I was front and center. But, for some strange reason, you can't teach an old dog new tricks.

"A woman for a captain?" I shouted. "That's not Picard!" You would think I would have learned from past mistakes, but once again, history repeated itself. In my mind, this new show was nothing more than a failed attempt to copy the success of *TNG*. It would never last. I stayed loyal to *Next Generation* right up until the bitter end. After that, as far as I was concerned, my *Trek*-watching days were over.

Years later, while working a job I affectionately referred to as "Hell on Earth," I made a lifestyle change. I decided to escape and pursue a career in writing; and so began my journey. Writing is a lonely job, as any writer will tell you. With all that time spent alone, it is sometimes hard to keep inspired. I needed something to fill the down time, to help expand my imagination and urge me to dream. So, with *TNG* reruns getting stale and nothing else on the glass teat to satisfy me, I decided to give *Voyager* its due.

And, inevitably, a few episodes later, I learned to love it too. *Voyager* not only brought my family together each week, but it always left me in a good mood — something unheard of in my youth.

I immediately began work on my masterpiece — my first movie script — and sent it off to Hollywood. Funny thing is, Hollywood had a different opinion than I, and my masterpiece is currently collecting dust in a box under my bed. To say I was devastated would be a bit of an understatement.

Feeling blue, sitting on my writer's block, I had visions of returning to Hell on Earth. That was when I heard of a *Star*

Trek convention taking place in Toronto, Canada. I had always heard stories of these things happening in Los Angeles or other far-off places I could never attend, but this was just two hours away. The guest of honor was none other than Jonathan Frakes. This was too good to be true. Being a starving writer, I started saving those pennies, and soon the big day arrived when I was off to my first convention.

When the doors opened, I casually walked inside, not knowing what to expect. That's about the time my jaw hit the floor. There was *Trek* as far as the eye could see and I was like a kid in a candy store. Even more important though was the opportunity to hear Mr. Frakes speak.

Sitting in the dark room, I anxiously awaited the man himself. After a video introduction and a standing ovation, Jonathan Frakes took the stage. At first I was a bit stunned. Not only was Mr. Frakes wearing blue jeans and sneakers, but he also had on this Hawaiian shirt and was sunburned. Jonathan "Wild Bill Riker" Frakes was a normal human being! This took a while to register, but it was true. He was very kind, answering questions about the show and telling stories from the set. He jokingly referred to Patrick Stewart as "Old Baldy," and was always smiling.

Then he did something that would change my way of looking at things. He started talking about the business side of the industry. He mentioned a project called *Roswell* that he was involved with, and told us that it was going to be canceled. He told us that he needed our support to stop this from happening. This shocked me. Why would someone like Mr. Frakes, a great actor, director, and producer, need our help? But as I would soon learn, even for someone like him, this industry is no bed of roses. He mentioned his early days as an actor, years

Jonathan Frakes at a fan convention (Photo courtesy Marc B. Lee)

before *TNG*, and this made me think of my current situation. If Mr. Frakes didn't start at the top, why did I think I could?

In *Star Trek*, nobody starts out as captain. They must first go to Starfleet academy, graduate, work as an ensign, move up in the ranks, and only then, through years of hard work and dedication, would they finally achieve their goal. I might have been out of the academy, but I was far from sitting in the captain's chair.

Waiting in line, I made some decisions that day. When my time came, I simply thanked Mr. Frakes for coming. He smiled that familiar smile I had seen so many times before, shook my hand, and thanked me for my support. Then he autographed a photo that hangs on my wall, beside the Brent Spiner one, as a reminder of what I had learned that day.

Starting over in my quest, I began at the bottom and have had nothing but success so far. I've written an independent short being produced, had articles published online, and continue to move up in the ranks. Someday I'll be a captain, but it is the journey that matters. The feeling you get from doing what you love for a living.

If I could go back in time (something totally feasible in the *Star Trek* universe), I would go to my teenage self and have a little talk. I wouldn't be angry or forceful, as *Trek* has taught me to take a more diplomatic approach to things. I would explain to him what I have learned, show him the errors of his ways . . . then stun him with my phaser for being so narrow-minded.

If you are reading this, then my first publication in novel form has come in the form of a short story in a book about *Star Trek*. How ironic is that?

I would like to thank Mr. Frakes for his honesty and insight; and thank you Gene Roddenberry, for creating a future we could look forward to, without hunger or greed, and inspiring us all to become better people.

A Wish Come True

BY ADAM BARGAR

In spring of 2000, I was 15 years old and diagnosed with testicular cancer. During the summer I underwent four courses of chemotherapy and three surgeries. Late in my treatment, the social worker at the Johns Hopkins Hospital told me that I would be eligible to receive a wish from the Make-A-Wish Foundation. I was initially reluctant, since I was not as sick as other children and knew I was going to be okay, and I thought I would be taking from resources that could be used for sicker kids. However, Make-A-Wish made it clear that I would not be, that cases like mine were what Make-A-Wish was founded for. So I decided that I wanted to go to L.A. and see *Voyager* being filmed.

These wishes take time, but as the months went by, I knew the show was going to end, and I was worried that the wish would not happen. But in late winter of 2000, I got a call from Make-A-Wish saying that I would be flying out in the last week of March. Best of all though, I got a call from Merri Howard's office saying that I would get a chance to be used as an extra on the series finale.

In L.A., I was fitted for my costume and the great folks at *Voyager* did my hair. When it was finally time to film, the experience was surreal. They were filming the episode "Endgame," and the scene where I make an appearance is the one where Admiral Janeway is lecturing a group of cadets in the future. I am sitting right next to the cadet who stands up and asks about "the look on the Borg Queen's face."

While I was on the set, I met Garrett Wang and Bob Picardo, and had a lengthy chat with Kate Mulgrew. Additionally, I got to tour all the sets (except the mess hall which had already been taken down) and Michael Westmore's makeup lab. The folks at *Voyager* were truly wonderful, and I got lots of screen time. My wish had truly been fulfilled!

Kids . . .

BY JAN WHITE

My story is not spectacular, just humorous. I have been a fan from the beginning, so I am one of the legion of middle-aged fans who still watch it. I consider myself a "Trekkie," since I have never gone to a convention, but do watch every episode at least once, and the VCR is set to tape the reruns in the middle of the night.

Mine is a generational story, since my children, now in their twenties, have been imbued with an appreciation of all things *Trek*, too. Around 10 years ago there was a *Star Trek* exhibit at the Air and Space Museum in Washington, D.C. My children were 10 and 13 years old. We were all having a great time bouncing about from display to display, and were on the bridge. When I sat in the Captain's chair, my very self-conscious 13-year-old son took a look around and got spooked.

He declared, "This is like that sketch on *Saturday Night Live*, everybody is a nerd here, and *I'm not a nerd*! All these guys have pocket protectors! I'm out of here!" We arranged to meet in a half hour at the gift shop.

A few years later, I accompanied my daughter, who was a teenager at the time, to the opening night of *First Contact*. We had to wait in line for about an hour to get into the multiplex, but even the line was fun. People were dressed in Starfleet uniforms, friendly and eager. After we settled in our seats, I went out to the concession stand. A huge man with long wavy hair and a fierce expression, dressed in studded leather, was striding into the theater, and I declared, "Heads up, the Klingons are here!" Everyone started laughing.

The audience in the movie was lively to say the least, and interacted with the story at appropriate places, but there was this one man behind us who had been commenting throughout the film, and had been taxing our patience with his noise during critical scenes. At the climax, when first contact was made, he mutters, "I bet it's Klingon." My daughter, who was very irritated by his rudeness by then, turned around and hissed, "Jerk! Can you *spell* 'Prime Directive'?" He sunk down in his seat, thoroughly chastened by a girl less than half his age. Someone said, "You go, kid!"

My son is still an avid but secretive fan. And my daughter still insists on going to opening nights for movies.

One thing that's often bothered me about non-Trekkers and non-sci-fi fans is their complete lack of understanding about all the charitable work that Star Trek *fans do. This story was just one of several I've included in this book that describe how the show has moved people to go out and make a difference in their community.*

Making a Difference

BY CHRISTOPHER J. LETO

I'm sure not very many people can tell you when and where they were when they became a Trekker.

I had known of the existence of *Star Trek* all my young life, but had never really much cared about it. I was an avid science fiction fan watching all the new shows that aired in the early part of the 1980s. I did watch *Star Trek* once in a while, but it was always the same episode: "Who Mourns For Adonis." I figured *Star Trek* must only be one episode, and a rather bad one at that.

Then one early evening I heard a rock hitting my window. My best friend from next door wanted to know if I wanted to go out to the cinema and see *Star Trek IV: The Voyage Home*. I wasn't really interested in seeing the movie, but I was bored, and it was a Friday night, so I decided I'd rather go out to a bad movie than stay in doing nothing. The problem was, I was only 15 years old. The movie would have let out way after my bedtime. My mother informed me that it was too late for me and that I should just go on Saturday to an earlier showing. I decided to go anyway.

It was the first defiant act of my teenage years. I am not sure why I did this. I had never disobeyed my mother before, nor had I really had any desire to see this movie. Nevertheless I sneaked out and went to see the film.

We arrived a half hour before the movie began and found ourselves waiting in line. I was amused and perhaps a little frightened to see grown adults dressed up as their favorite Starfleet officers and aliens. They were loud and in good cheer, yelling out their favorite episodes, quoting their favorite characters and bonding with each other. In rather Vulcan-like fashion I scoffed at them and felt pity for these adults who were acting, in my opinion, like mentally deficient children.

I sat in the theater next to a man who was probably in his mid-twenties, and he asked me about my favorite episodes of *Star Trek*. I had to confess that I had never seen an episode or any of the three previous movies. He was quite shocked and began to summarize what had happened in the previous three films. I had no idea that I was walking into the middle of a story.

The lights went down, the cheering began, and the movie started. I was instantly hooked. The characters were so alive, the story fun and interesting. After that movie ended, suddenly the people around me didn't seem as foolish. I left that theater wanting to know everything there was to know about this show.

On the way back from the cinema I stopped at a drug store and found the *Star Trek IV* novelization and purchased it. That was just the beginning. During the next several months I bought every *Star Trek* novel that had ever been published, all the videocassettes and movies, and subscribed to the newsletter. I became a fanatic.

I did not know at the age of 15 what I had wanted to do with my life, but after consuming *Star Trek*, I knew that whatever it was, I wanted to make a difference.

I think with the help of *Star Trek* I did make a difference. When I was 21 I joined an Environmental Agency to help work on local issues and my boss turned out to be the same person in the movie theater who had given me the backstory on *Star Trek*. After the Environmental Agency I worked at United Cerebral Palsy, working with people who had disabilities. I then moved onto a program at the United Nations that helped foreign countries rebuild or start small businesses to stabilize their economy.

To this day I watch the shows and read all the books and while perhaps my desire to spend every penny I earn has waned a bit, my love of what *Star Trek* represents is just as strong as ever.

The Continuing Mission . . . in Singapore

BY KELVIN W. LIM

Someone once asked me, "What do you like about *Star Trek*? There are no lightsabers, too much unintelligible conversations, and nine unremarkable movies!" At some time in every Trekker's life, we have all had to defend our faith in a 35-year-old series that is associated with fervent, bespectacled geeks. This is my response to those skeptics and a short tale of my baptism into Trekdom.

My voyage to where no one has gone before and beyond began at Tower Books, with an impromptu purchase of the *Star Trek: Generations* computer game. At that point in time, I was unemployed and had spent many afternoons by the mailbox, awaiting letters from prospective employers. It was a depressing period in my life, and I was in desperate need of intellectual stimulation. Also, something about Patrick Stewart's steely gaze mesmerized me. Out of curiosity, I bought it.

The game introduced numerous foreign, intriguing elements such as the tricorder and the Klingons. But, most importantly, it removed me from the depths of desolation, and transported me to numerous strange, fascinating planets. My mind reeled from the journey across space and time.

And that was the beginning of an enterprising search for all forms of *Trek* literature and paraphernalia. A whole new world beckoned me, and I readily plunged into this vast wealth of make believe. In less than six months, I read over 60 *Star Trek* novels and assembled a modest museum at home.

The biggest obstacle for me was in comprehending the

technobabble, but that was easily overshadowed by the depth of the storytelling, the vast array of equipment, the wonderful assortment of aliens, the beautiful starships, and the *Deep Space Nine* station. I thoroughly enjoyed the films, especially *The Voyage Home*, *First Contact*, *Insurrection*, and even the much maligned *The Final Frontier*, which I remember fondly for the scene where Sybok explored Spock and Doctor McCoy's past.

But nothing compares to the introduction to Gates McFadden. I fell in love with this incredible actress who, in spite of the cruelly limited screen exposure, brilliantly portrays the captain's better half and the ever-reliable Chief Medical Officer. The sensual "Sub Rosa" is one of my favorite episodes.

My most memorable *Trek* experience happened at the *Star Trek* World Tour. Organized by Messe Dusseldorf Asia in collaboration with Paramount Pictures, it came to town in early December 1999. From the *Star Trek* Museum to Quark's Bazaar, and an exciting adventure aboard a realistically constructed replica of the Starship *Enterprise*, we were dazzled by the exquisite props and the professionalism of the actors. With the simulated transporter experience, the blinking lights on all the consoles and Q's "accompanying presence" on our adventure/tour in the ship, we were plunged into a world that we had come to embrace and long for!

It was a phenomenal experience that I will never forget because it literally cemented my lifelong membership in the *Trek* fraternity. On that fateful day, my girlfriend and I were on the bridge of the *Enterprise*, which was under attack by the menacing Borg. The actors entertained us with their incredibly professional portrayal of a starship crew working together to battle the enemy and save the ship. Suddenly, the captain ran up to us (the audience) and led *me* to the most coveted chair in film history. I was too dumbstruck to give the command to fire at the Borg cube (it was destroyed eventually), and all I could do was savor that moment in the captain's chair. I can still remember the feel of my hands on the plastic-framed consoles, and the view of the bridge and the viewscreen.

For that brief moment in time, I was the Captain of the *Enterprise.*

Sometimes, I will gaze up at the sky and think that maybe . . . just maybe . . . there is a starship orbiting our planet or a distant space station housing unusual and fearsome life forms. At times when I am troubled, I remember the problems that my heroes faced (some of which make mine look trivial!) and the way they overcame them with fortitude, integrity, and intelligence. This convinces me that I can do the same. Similarly, I draw strength and purpose from the way Captains Picard and Sisko handle the loneliness of command. I hope that, someday, when I find myself in a similar situation, I may draw on their example and earn the respect of my teammates/colleagues.

Star Trek is television's finest hour and I have learned much from the crews of the *Enterprise* and *Deep Space Nine* — courage, integrity, leadership, friendship, and loyalty. The mission continues, and *Star Trek* will live on in my heart and mind. This insatiable appetite for all things *Trek* made me the person I am today and I am proud to proclaim — I AM A TREKKER.

Three Generations of Trekkers

BY RYAN MOORE

The group of friends with whom I attend conventions and *Trek* events often get asked, "How long have you been watching *Star Trek*?" Most answer, "Since the third season of *Next Generation*," or "fourth season of *DS9*," but I'm one of the proud few who can say, "I started watching *Next Generation* from the very first episode."

In fact, I began watching earlier than that. I started down the Great Roddenberry Road when I was around eight or nine years old. I was playing in my bedroom when I heard my father call out, "Hey Ryan! Come in here! There's something on TV you'll like!" It was then that my father introduced me to *Star Trek*; more specifically, to a rerun of *The Original Series*.

To my amazement, my father knew everything that was going to happen in the show. Soon after this I was pestering him about when *Star Trek* would be on; I had become a first-class *Trek* mark in short order. We'd watch it together — we *always* watched it together. And he'd always know what was going to happen. The reason he knew was simple — he'd watched all the episodes before as a teenager, with *his* father. So, when a new *Trek* movie came out, the three of us went together.

To me, *Star Trek* is more than just a television show with a huge fan community encompassing it; it is a tradition in my family and a link to those who have come before me. My father and grandfather are men of exceptional courage, integrity, and character; whenever I see a Starfleet emblem or a picture of a young William Shatner in a gold command uniform, I always think of my father and grandfather, and it reminds me of where I came from, and who I am.

Real Life: The Final Frontier

BY MARK EMANUEL MENDOZA

The impact of this great show on the development of my own life began back in 1966 when both *Star Trek* and I were born. My father and uncle were fans of *The Original Series* and my earliest recollections were of sitting and watching it with them. My love for science fiction began almost immediately. Not just any science fiction, mind you, but specifically *Star Trek*. You see, this show taught me as a pup how to be a member of a team and how cultural diversity is an advantage, not something to be feared.

As *Star Trek* entered syndication, I entered elementary school. A funny thing happens with syndication. In El Paso, *Star Trek* ran at approximately 4 p.m., immediately after school. I would rush home to turn on the TV and watch the exploits of my dear friends Captain Kirk, Commander Spock, and Dr. McCoy. My friends and I would play act *Star Trek* at school. My favorite expression when I was in the third grade was, "Fascinating," and I had the Vulcan salute down as if I had been born there.

It was during this time that I also developed command skills, the ability to think on my feet, and a sense of fair play and justice, just like a certain ship's captain from Iowa. I learned that it is all right to disagree with friends, sometimes vehemently, and still be friends just like Bones and Spock. The reason for this type of life learning, I firmly believe, is that *Star Trek* is not really science fiction. It takes place in space and there are Klingons and Gorn to deal with, but I fervently believe that *Star Trek* is *LIFE*. The virtues and skills taught by this landmark piece of Americana are ones that helped develop leadership and humanity and continue to do so. In our daily lives, are not fair play and justice still the ideal? Do we all not have to deal with our own personal Klingons and Romulans?

As the years progressed, I watched as a well known crew reunited as a family would to confront the dangers of V'Ger and the like. I learned about non-violent conflict resolution, interpersonal relations, and the importance of having a crew that relates as family members and not strangers. I watched as the death of a dear friend and teacher was faced with strength and dignity by crew and audience alike. I watched as a captain risked all, including his ship and his son, for the life of a friend. I even

Patrick Stewart (Photo courtesy Marc B. Lee)

developed a newfound love of nature in the form of a pair of cetaceans called George and Gracie. I learned that former enemies could be converted into trusted allies with a little work.

All of this was formative knowledge for me as I studied to be exactly what *Star Trek* indeed is: a teacher. But something even more fantastic happened as I entered the field of elementary education. A new teacher known as Star *Trek: The Next Generation* was born! During this time I was experiencing classroom life for the first time and was also studying to be a school principal. During the ensuing seven years, I learned about measured response to a crisis. I learned about conference evaluations and the importance of listening to the advice and expertise of the people under my command and making an informed decision. I learned about command with compassion and striving for excellence at all times. I learned about the advantages of having a diverse command crew, each with his or her own talents and limitations. Further, the most important lesson I learned, given two tremendous captains and role models to study, is that no one command style is the best one. Depending on the situation, one must be Kirk, Spock, Picard, Riker, or a combination of all of them.

Shortly thereafter two more teachers were born in the form of *Deep Space Nine* and *Voyager*. From Sisko I learned of the passion of commitment to a higher purpose and that at times it is necessary to do not only what is right according to policy, but what is just plain right. I learned how to start a station from scratch and how to take isolated, disenfranchised personnel and make a team out of them. And from another teacher, Kathryn Janeway, I learned how to make tough decisions, whatever the personal costs. Most importantly, I learned that a commander can and should care about his or her crew. Tough decisions still need to be made, but they should be made humanely, taking into consideration caring and the trust of those people in one's charge.

My name is Mark Emanuel Mendoza and I currently serve the El Paso Independent School District as the Principal at LTC William Bliss Elementary School, the top school in the district. It gives me great pride to say that I was born and raised in Gene Roddenberry's hometown and I take his vision of the future as my marching orders.

In the field I have chosen, I have the honor and privilege of impacting the lives of thousands of people from teachers to students to the community. I believe that the best way to develop the future is the Roddenberry way. The key to the future is knowledge. But much more so than knowledge, a person should have insight and enlightenment. I believe that the characters we have all come to know personally and to love are so important to us because they are all part of every one of us. My job is to teach my students to be Data and to start them on a mission of discovery for the rest of their lives. You see, *Star Trek* is what life is all about!

Pleased to Meet You

When I first asked for stories from fans, I expected to hear a lot of stories about meeting the actors and writers from the show at conventions. When the various stories began pouring in, I was amazed at the different ways fans met the actors. While the majority did meet them at conventions (and I've put those stories in a separate chapter on convention experiences), I received one story by a man who runs a cable access show in Rhode Island and has interviewed several *Trek* stars; one by a woman who met Patrick Stewart on a ship when he was filming *Moby Dick*; one by a fan who met a guest star at a charity event; and another by a woman who ran into Robert Picardo in Las Vegas. While I received a couple of very well written stories about unfortunate experiences meeting the stars (where the celebrities were rude), I decided not to run them because I wanted to maintain the positive aspect of the celebrities from *Star Trek*. After all, you just have to appear on one episode and we'll worship you forever. So read on, and see just how gracious the actors on *Star Trek* have been to the fans.

One of my favorite submissions was from Barry Cook, who runs a cable access show in Rhode Island called "Star Trek: The Unofficial Fan Club Show." *His original submission was shorter, but once I prodded him for more information, he came up with a bunch of great stories of the best guests he's had on the show.*

Tales from the Land of Cable Access

BY BARRY COOK

I was born too late to catch the series' original run, but I became a huge fan in the '70s. In 1993, after I tried and failed for two years to use my communications degree to get a job in television, I decided I needed some experience and maybe some notoriety to help me get a job. So, I put on a statewide cable television public access show and used *Trek* as a topic because it was my biggest area of knowledge. It was a very simple show: I and a co-host in my living room just talking about *Trek*. I called it *Star Trek: The Unofficial Fan Club Show*. Only in my fantasies did I believe this would actually amount to anything, and that we'd even get noticed. In the show's outline I even included that from time to time we would interview *Trek* actors who came to local conventions, only half believing it would ever happen. Well, to my surprise, we were instantly popular, a cult favorite. We immediately began to get mail almost daily. Not a ton, but one or two pieces a day.

On the show, we gave *Trek* news, displayed new products, showed clips of *Trek* actors in other things, old and new, and covered conventions. In our second episode, we got an interview with Walter Koenig at a con in Massachusetts, and over the years have interviewed Nana Visitor, Robin Curtis, Majel Barrett Roddenberry, George Takei, all the men of *Voyager*, René Auberjonois, Michael Dorn and Terry Farrell together, Gary Lockwood, Frank Goershin, Leonard Nimoy, Roberta Lenard (daughter of Mark), and D.C. Fontana.

The show has been going for eight years now, with a new episode once a month. We are recognized in public all the time. We make no money at this and do it as a labor of love for ourselves and the fans. There is no way I can convey on paper how amazing this journey has been, and so many cool things have happened throughout the years.

The Roberta Lenard story is particularly nice because of the emotional level at the time, and because Roberta shared many personal stories about her dad with us as well as family photos. It was two months after her dad Mark, the actor who played Sarek, had died of cancer. She let us into her apartment in Sommerville, MA, and was very kind to us. She almost cried at several moments while talking about her father, and it created some very emotional and powerful moments. She showed us photos from her album as well as some photo collages she had made after his death that were very spiritual in nature. She spoke of him as a young man and of her mother and of her own experiences on *Trek* sets with him. She spoke of his friend-

Mark Lenard in Edmonton, Canada.
(Photo courtesy Pat Whittaker)

ship with Walter Koenig and of hers with Nichelle Nichols. She introduced us to her roommate and asked us to stay for dinner, but we had to get back to Rhode Island. A technical assistant on our show said that he found it to be so moving that he almost went to the phone to make a donation because it gave him the same feeling as one of those telethons. We also made up a tribute montage of clips from Mark's *Star Trek* appearances with dramatic music. It ran with the interview. I sent a copy of the episode to Roberta and she showed it to her mother and siblings. Roberta later told me that they were all very moved by the montage. Hearing that was probably the single greatest moment in the show's history for me. Roberta is a friend to the show to this day. I call her on her dad's birthday every year to let her know we are all thinking of her father and her family. She is a very cool person.

When Leonard Nimoy was in town, many media outlets wanted to interview him, including the local news stations, newspapers, and my public access competition. He was in Massachusetts and Rhode Island over a two-day period, and no one got to interview him but me.

We waited all day for him to finish his appearance at the convention in Boston he had attended with William Shatner. When we got in the convention green room, it was just my co-host, the cameraman, a convention company representative, Nimoy, and me. My co-host and I each took a chair on one side of him. I could see his eyes behind his glasses at an angle, and they looked tired. It was an interesting moment because it made him so real to me. As long as I had been doing this kind of thing, these actors still awed me.

I asked him a couple of questions, one of which was, "What do you like most and least about Mr. Spock, and what would he say he liked most and least about Leonard Nimoy?" He kind of chuckled and said, "That's a personal question," and I apologized. He then answered only the first part of the question. He said there wasn't anything about Spock he didn't like.

In December 2000 we interviewed Terry Farrell (Dax) at a con in New York. We got to the convention center early, and were setting up the room when Terry walked in. Usually, a convention rep and a personal assistant accompany the actors, so I didn't pay any attention to who was with her. I

Leonard Nimoy considers a fan's question. (Photo courtesy Marc B. Lee)

looked up quickly, saw her, and went into host mode. But then I heard Terry talking to herself out loud explaining that she had forgotten about the interview but was ready to sit down and do it. Then I heard this booming voice say, "Oh, you have an interview?" and I looked up. Well, I nearly fell

Michael Dorn addresses the audience at FEDCON 8. (Photo courtesy Susanne Dörfler)

over because it was none other than . . . Michael Dorn! He introduced himself and shook my hand and then said something to the effect that he would go ahead and get out of the way and I said, "No no no! That's okay! We weren't expecting you, but you're a bonus. Please sit down!" I pulled up a chair for him and he did! They were very friendly to us. Especially Terry. I point that out because a lot of the time the actors are tired when they get to us and while they are usually pretty pleasant and jocular, they are not always super-friendly and warm. Terry and Michael were warm to each other too, and their chemistry as friends was very apparent on camera. They joked back and forth with each other and it was just a great interview.

The story of the George Takei interview is interesting. I called his agent and faxed the request to George at his home using a local mail/copy/fax services shop. I called them later that day to see if he had responded and I almost choked on the bite of sandwich I was chomping when they said he had. I went to pick it up and my hands were shaking the whole way. (This was early in the show's history, I should mention.) He had agreed to the interview with the proviso that we keep it short because he was traveling with his mom to a book signing in Providence, which was where I was going to have to catch up with him. The bookstore he went to was very small, so we had to walk up the street to the lobby of a small second-run art film theater less than a block away to do the interview. It was cool because it was mid-summer and all the college kids, many *Trek* fans among them, were all hanging out on the street in the cafés and shops and here I was with George Takei — Mr. Sulu — and his bodyguard, walking up the street in broad daylight. How cool is that?

Rhode Island is a small state, so for us, this kind of "fame" is a big deal and for the local *Trek* fans, the idea that two guys from their little home state could gain access to the actors and bring home interviews is a huge deal. It has given us a feeling of connection with the show and the *Trek* vibe that most fans do not get to experience. And as far as I know, no other television show like mine exists.

If you'd like to contact the show, you can do so at STTUFCLUB@aol.com

PLEASED TO MEET YOU

Sailing with the Captain

BY CAROL TAYLOR

I have been involved with the Australian sailing ship, the Alma Doepel, since 1995. My great-great uncle was the ship's master in 1917, so sailing has been in our family for many generations. The vessel, which had her first sail in 1903, has been used for private weekend cruises, tours, and filming. I had been volunteering with the ship for two years when it was announced that a film crew was going to be filming *Moby Dick* on the ship, and they needed volunteers to help the cast and train them in how to run a ship. I heard that Patrick Stewart was going to be one of the actors, and I volunteered immediately. I didn't care that it would be a week's work without pay: I had been watching

Patrick Stewart on the Alma Doepel with Carol Taylor. (Photo courtesy Carol Taylor)

Star Trek since the beginning of *The Next Generation*, and I think Patrick is as sexy as Sean Connery. When the opportunity arrived for a chance to meet him face-to-face I just jumped at it. Who wouldn't?

I was involved in the training of the cast for the movie to make them look more authentic in their roles. Patrick came on one of these days to check out how the training was progressing. I ended up spending 15 minutes with him alone while I was on helm duty (steering the ship) and was able to talk to him, uninterrupted for that time. I didn't really go into how much of a fan I was; I didn't want to scare him off by harping about it. The gist of the conversation was about my involvement with the sailing ship, her history of sailing, and as a youth-sail training vessel.

If I lose all other memories, I know I will not forget that day. It was the highlight of my sailing career.

Arresting Krull

BY STEPHANIE SMITH

I am a member of a local Klingon club called House K'ralvaj, and Starfest 2001 in April was one that I don't think many of us will forget. Some of our members run The Brig, an attraction where someone is "arrested" and they try to raise enough money for "bail." The money goes to charity, and on Saturday someone got the bright idea to arrest Cary-Hiroyuki Tagawa, a former *Next Generation* guest star who was there to promote his new movie, *Planet of the Apes*. Cary took it all in stride, even going so far as to do this funny ape imitation while sitting in the Brig, and not only did he pose for pictures with members of the House when he got out, he gave one of the younger members an "ape-back" ride around the Activities Room. Now a lot of stars might not do that, but Mr. Tagawa really had fun and so did the kid. I have to give him major points for that.

I wasn't sure at first whether or not to include this story, since it might strike a nerve with Trekkers who are big fans of Voyager*, but it was a good story about how the Internet has provided fans with a way to interact with the writers directly.*

The Producer Trekkers Love to Hate

BY REZA SHIRALY

Brannon Braga, co-producer of *Voyager* and writer of over 50 *Star Trek* episodes (as well as two of the films) is often referred to as the producer *Star Trek* fans love to hate. In the eyes of the fans, his downfall began way back in 1994 when *Star Trek VII: Generations* came out. For one reason or another, it was assumed that he and Rick Berman (who co-wrote the film with him) were responsible for the death of Captain Kirk. Then, the final blow came with *Voyager*. While I realize it's a popular series with many Trekkers, I believe the writers didn't take advantage of the show's full potential, and the characterization of Seven of Nine was an insult to fans. This Borg in a catsuit, turning *Star Trek* into *Borgwatch*, overshadowed the authority of Captain Janeway; it seemed like every other episode was about Seven of Nine! Mr. Braga later admitted that this happened because it was simply easier for the writers to write for her. Many blame him for the defanging of the Borg. In *TNG*, the Borg were ruthless and scary — on *Voyager*, they *negotiated*! Mind you, all of this occurred after Braga took the reins on *Voyager* during season three.

Then, Ronald D. Moore, a long time writer-turned-producer on *DS9* went on to write for *Voyager* with his then-best friend Brannon Braga. He quit after a very short time, and shortly thereafter gave a substantial interview to a *Trek* Web site saying why he quit. This man basically developed most of what we know about the Klingon world, and when he went on to say what Braga was doing to *Voyager* and the franchise (treating writers badly, instructing them to overlook continuity), fans got very upset.

I personally found Mr. Braga to be a nice guy, just misunderstood. He is a good writer. Along with Moore, he wrote *Star Trek VIII: First Contact* — one of the most popular *Trek* movies. He also co-wrote the finale of *TNG*, again with Moore. He is a good writer . . . most of the time. We need to forget the past (*Voyager*) and focus on the present (*Enterprise*).

A good six months before fans knew anything about *Enterprise*, there was a news story on a *Trek* site that Brannon Braga, the man who was co-creating the series, had registered a domain name. I was very bored that day so I went over to the domain-registering site and signed up so I could get access to the contact info on those who had registered names. I requested the info for his site and sure enough, I got an e-mail with Mr. Braga's AOL screenname (and e-mail address), his office address, and office number. I too happened to be an AOL member so I placed Mr. Braga on my "buddy-list," so that I would know when we both were online.

The next day, we both were. I sent him an Instant Message a couple of times with no luck. I thought I had to say something that would get his attention. So I did; I told him I knew who was leaking info on upcoming *Trek* episodes, which was true, to some extent. I knew the alias of one such informant and I gave it to him and he thanked me. Over the next two months, I would send him an IM every time some kind of "spoiler" made its way onto the Net. For the most part, all I got back was an "Interesting," or "It always amazes me how fans get this info." But, there were those days where he would ask my opinion on "spoilers." When the script for "Broken Bow" was on the Internet, and I told him, the first thing he said was, "What do you think?" I proceeded to give him my review.

My fondest memory of our short "chats" occurred when I told him a classic *Star Trek* joke that I thought he would already know. You know, the one about Captain Kirk and toilet paper (how they both go around Uranus looking for Klingons). He laughed and laughed and said he would pass it on to Rick Berman.

Although he never told me any info on *Enterprise* (he did give me some phony episode titles that we both knew were fake), I enjoy our little "chats." Even today, we still talk on AOL at least once every other week. He usually asks me what I thought about the previous week's episode. I am proud to say that I am, in a small and humble way, "friends" with the producer Trekkers love to hate.

Frankly, Scarlett . . .

BY MANDI BOHN

When Scarlett Pomers first appeared on *Voyager* as Naomi

Wildman in 1998, I immediately thought that she was a very talented young girl. I began frequenting her official Web site, made a fanpage of my own, and joined her fan club on Yahoo. When I found out I'd be taking a trip to L.A. in the summer of '99, I asked Scarlett's Webmaster, with whom I'd been exchanging e-mails, if there was any possibility that I might be able to meet her while there. Before I knew it, it was August 12, 1999, and I was waiting at the entrance to the tram tour ride at Universal Studios, where I had arranged to meet Scarlett.

I was very nervous about what I was going to say or what she'd think of me. I was afraid that I'd be too shy to say any-

Mandi Bohn meets Scarlett Pomers. (Photo courtesy Mandi Bohn)

thing and we wouldn't have anything to talk about. When Scarlett arrived, she walked right up to me, extended her hand, and said with a smile, "Are you Mandi?" And I knew right away that there was nothing to be afraid of.

Both Scarlett, who was 10 years old at the time, and her mother were very friendly and talkative. Scarlett had brought me an autographed picture, and was all too happy to pose for a few pictures with me. We got on the tram tour ride, and she pointed out special places along the way, including the building where she'd done her first job at age three. I was very impressed with both her and her mother for their friendliness and courtesy. I spent about an hour with Scarlett that day, and when she had to go, she shook my hand once more saying that it had been fun to spend time with me. I don't think I'll ever meet another little girl as kind or as special as Scarlett Pomers.

Having Dinner with the Doc

BY STACEY HOROWITZ

On Saturday, April 28, 2001, I attended an autograph session with Robert Picardo at *Star Trek: The Experience* in the Hilton hotel in Las Vegas. I waited in line like everyone else and decided to go into Quark's Bar to quench my thirst. To my surprise, Picardo sat down next to me and began to eat a plate of weird looking pot stickers that he openly commented on. He was extremely friendly and started a conversation with me. When I informed him that I've appreciated his work since being on *China Beach*, he told me his friend Megan Gallagher was getting married and that he was there in Las Vegas to attend the bachelor party. To my surprise, he was very down to earth and inspiring.

My mother (the ultimate Trekkie) had always wanted to write a *Star Trek* novel, and after she died I began writing a *Voyager* novel in my spare time. I was pleased when Mr. Picardo autographed it for me. Meeting the "EMH" has motivated me to getting my story completed. I'm grateful to him for allowing me to fulfill a dream that I share with my late mother.

One of the most enthusiastic submitters was Jonathan Lane. He sent me so many different submissions — and I wanted to include all of them (I limited myself to four). This guy is definitely one of the most serious Trekkers I've ever talked to, and I hope you enjoy his stories. However, I wouldn't recommend trying to do what he did in this next piece: we wouldn't want Paramount stopping a bunch of fans with this book under their arm as a how-to guide to sneaking around the Star Trek *sets . . .*

Sneaking onto the Voyager Sets

BY JONATHAN LANE

In *Star Trek* fandom, it's not what you know so much as who you know . . . and how many favors you can get from them. It's also about taking a few risks while not doing anything too stupid.

My good friend Lisa Mueller is a convention organizer on the East Coast who occasionally involves herself in entrepreneurial science-fiction ventures. Back in the summer of 1996, Lisa was creating a series of phone cards featuring various sci-fi actors, and she was out in L.A. to collect some contract signatures from a few of them, including Tim Russ (Tuvok). Tim had suggested that Lisa drive over to Paramount Studios in Hollywood and meet him on the *Voyager* sets where he'd sign his contract.

Lisa was staying at my apartment for the week, and I graciously offered to drive her to Paramount. And of course, I told her I could escort her onto the sets. (Wasn't I generous?) Lisa was more than happy to take me along; it would be her first time at Paramount Studios. I decided to bring along a camera with extra film and batteries — just in case — although I knew they'd never let us take pictures.

Tim Russ left us a "drive-on" pass at the main Melrose Avenue gate, meaning we could park in the Paramount lot. Then we walked over to Soundstage 8, where *Voyager* filmed. We looked for Tim's trailer, found it, and knocked on the door. No answer. Maybe he was actually on the soundstage? We wandered slowly toward the entrance, scared we might be somewhere we weren't supposed to be.

The entrance to Stage 8 was pretty unassuming. Nothing said "Voyager" on it, and it looked like just another doorway into a small room, with another doorway leading into the main soundstage itself. Someone came out. "Excuse us, is Tim Russ in there?" we asked. "We were supposed to meet him."

"I'm not sure," the person answered. "You might want to go inside and look for him."

Wow, pretty tight security, huh? Whether intended or not, we took that as our invitation, and in we went.

If you've never been to a Hollywood soundstage, two things will hit you immediately: the size and the temperature. Soundstages can be half the size of a football field or larger.

Most soundstages are essentially just huge, empty spaces made up of four walls, a floor, and a ceiling about three to four storeys high. Inside, sets are built and laid out next to each other in what seems like a disorganized mess. Most soundstages are freezing cold, and this one was no exception. The reason for the frigid temperature is because, when filming, the lights can get very hot, and actors can be under them for quite a while. Having the temperature set low keeps most actors from sweating profusely under the lights during their scenes.

So in we walked, our hearts pounding out of our chests. This was it! We were about to see the sets of the *U.S.S. Voyager*! Or would some uniformed security officer stop us just inches away from our "holy grail"? We held our breath and turned a corner into the vastness of the humungous soundstage.

There was no one there. No one. It was 11:15 a.m. on a Thursday; you'd think someone would be working. We kept walking towards something that looked like . . . was it? It was! The Bridge of the *U.S.S. Voyager* was directly in front of us! You could look right in, as the part of the set containing the view screen was not in place, leaving a large gap. It was surreal. Here was the nerve center of one of the Federation's most advanced starships, yet if you took a step back, you'd see plywood and wiring surrounding this futuristic image.

I looked around to see if anyone could see us. My pulse racing, I reached into my bag, pulled out my camera, and took a quick photo. Flash! Click. I rushed to put the camera back in my bag. Would we be jumped by 20 armed security guards? We waited, looking around nervously.

Nothing happened. We started breathing again.

"Well, I guess Tim's not here," I said. "Maybe we ought to

The set of the U.S.S. Voyager Bridge. (Photo courtesy Jonathan Lane)

look around for him." This strategy would accomplish two things: 1) it would allow us to explore more of the sets, and 2) it would move us away from where I'd taken the flash photo, just in case the Paramount police were on their way.

We wandered onto a set built away from the others, a set with its own ceiling built over the top of it. Stepping inside, Lisa and I were suddenly in the Mess Hall. All of the seats and tables were covered in clear plastic (to keep them clean), and there was a twentieth-century garbage can sitting on Neelix's kitchen counter. Looking out of the "windows" (which were just open spaces — no glass), we discovered what space is really made of: black velvet with tiny rhinestone studs glued on.

The velvet is stretched out between two rollers like an old parchment scroll. As the ship travels through space at sublight speeds, the velvet is slowly rolled horizontally. When the ship is traveling at warp speed, a green screen replaces the velvet rolls, and the star-streaking effects of a warp-field are digitally composited into the scene.

We were essentially surrounded on all sides by walls and a ceiling. Taking a chance, I whipped out the camera once more and snapped another flash photo. Again, I quickly hid the camera back in my bag. Hearts racing, we waited again for the dire consequences of our heinous actions. Again, nothing happened.

"Hey, Lisa, why don't you stand over by the kitchen area and pose for a shot?" I got out my camera again. Flash! Click. This time I put my camera back more casually. "Wanna go back to the Bridge?" Lisa asked, smiling.

Back at the Bridge, I took out my camera again, this time composing a nicer shot where you could see the inside of the set as well as the plywood on the outside. With no one around, we stepped up onto the Bridge itself and started to look around. We would discover later that we were particularly fortunate that day in that all of the panel lights had been turned on in preparation for filming that afternoon. So not only were we seeing the Bridge, but it was all lit up with glowing consoles and everything! These displays are so detailed, that in the side-view *Voyager* Engineering cutaway schematic that lights up behind the captain's chair, you can actually see little black dots that represent the turbolifts traveling back and forth and up and down throughout the ship.

As we walked around the Bridge, looking closely at all the consoles, we suddenly had company. A wiring guy had walked onto the Bridge set to check something. We decided to take the initiative, so I turned to him and said, "Hi there. Tim Russ told us to wait for him here. Is it okay if we look around while we wait?"

The guy looked at us with a shrug and said, "Hey, I don't know you who you are, and I don't care. Do whatever."

Ah, Hollywood! *If it doesn't affect me directly, then I don't care.* I love this town!

He walked away and we continued to gawk. I pulled out the camera again. I took a picture of Lisa sitting at the Science Station. She took one of me in Tom Paris's chair at the Helm. I took one of her in front of the bronze *U.S.S. Voyager* plaque. And so it went at every Bridge station. We even both sat in

At the Helm of the Voyager. (Photo courtesy Jonathan Lane)

Chakotay's chair. (For some reason, we just couldn't bring ourselves to sit in the actual Captain's chair.) To be honest, those chairs weren't very comfortable, and they were kind of flimsy. In fact, I accidentally pulled the armrest off Chakotay's chair! (Fortunately, it snapped right back into place, but I believe my heart stopped momentarily.)

Having exhausted all photo opportunities on the Bridge, and with my camera now hanging around my neck, we decided to see what it was like in the turbolift. Expecting to enter a small, enclosed area, we were surprised to discover the inside of the turbolift was missing a wall. You could walk out the side of the turbolift to the open area behind the Bridge set . . . and we did. In fact, we took a few more steps and walked through a doorway into a completely different set: the Transporter Room!

Oh, this was just getting better and better. Like the Mess Hall, the Transporter Room was completely enclosed, with walls on all sides and a ceiling. We took close-up photos of the panel displays. We took shots of each other on the Transporter platform and standing at the Transporter control console. What would be next?

We walked out the same door we entered and headed further away from the Bridge. Turning a corner, we were suddenly walking along a *Voyager* corridor. The carpets lining the corridor were among the softest we'd ever stood on, and the carpet was completely covered with clear plastic to protect it.

Not wanting to miss anything, we walked through the first door off the corridor and right into Sickbay. I stood at a medical console while Lisa sat on the chair in the Doctor's office. I struck a pose next to a floor fan that was just sitting there in front of the bio-beds. Kneeling down and putting my arm

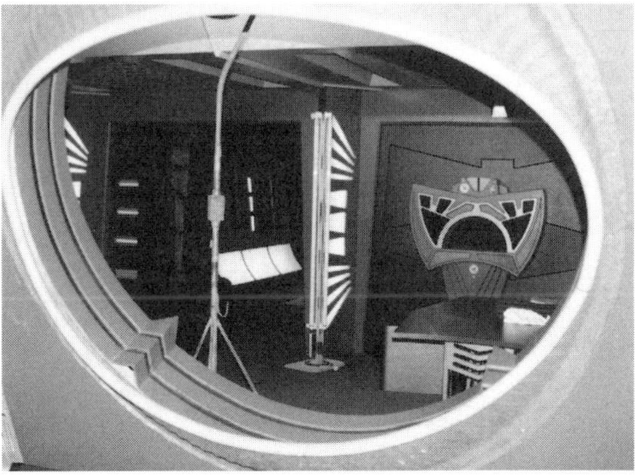

(Top) Crewman Lane prepares to beam down; (Middle) Keeping the dust away: this generic set was used for multiple locations, from Voyager science labs to alien control rooms; (Bottom) A view from outside the station: here we take a look through a "window" into one of the crew quarters of Deep Space Nine. (Photos courtesy Jonathan Lane)

around the floor fan, I had Lisa take a photo that I like to call, "*Star Trek* fans."

Ahem.

Lisa actually got up onto one of the bio-beds, where I took her picture. I thought about doing this myself, but I'm 220 pounds. Remembering what had happened with Chakotay's armrest, I decided not to risk sitting or lying down on one of the beds. They felt really flimsy and delicate. And Lisa said they were flat, hard, and not at all comfortable.

After Sickbay, we returned to the corridor and walked further along until we came to a wide opening. The corridor continued, but the walls on one side were gone, opening into a clear area of the soundstage where a number of people seemed to be having a meeting. We didn't want to risk being seen, but we'd already been everywhere behind us. We wanted to see more. Getting our courage up, I put my camera back into my bag. The crowd of people was about 20 feet away, and we walked calmly, trying not to make eye contact and looking like we knew where we were going. As soon as we passed the open area, we ducked through another side door. We were now in Engineering.

As awesome as the other sets had been, Engineering was even more so. All we could see in any direction was Engineering. It was like standing in the actual Engineering section on *Voyager*, not just a set. The ceiling around the warp core (which was not glowing and looked like just a gray metal column) was two storeys high. All of the panels were lit and blinking, and there were a lot of them. The set was so huge that when I got my photos developed later, only the close-up shots of Engineering came out. The long shots were too dark because my little fill-flash wasn't strong enough to light up the entire room.

The warp core in Engineering. (Photo courtesy Jonathan Lane)

As we gawked at our most awesome set yet, three people walked in, being led by a fourth. Hopefully, it was just a production crewmember giving some friends a tour. Taking our cue from the guy we'd seen on the Bridge, we tried to look like we were supposed to be there, just walking around. "Hey there," we both said, smiling, and gave a short wave. "Hello," they responded and proceeded to ignore us.

Having shot half a roll of film on Engineering alone (and, no, we didn't go upstairs because we couldn't find a way up), we wandered back down the corridor to the end, where we discovered a little room that we suspected hadn't been used for a while. What wasn't covered in plastic was covered in dust. I think it was the generic laboratory/alien bridge set that always seems to look slightly similar with subtle changes depending on how they decorate it.

By this point we had visited every set we could find inside that soundstage. There might have been more, but we didn't know where to look. I had just started my third roll of film and was dying to take more photos. "Wanna try to sneak onto *Deep Space Nine*?" I asked, knowing the *DS9* sets were right across the "street" on Stage 4. Lisa smiled a hungry grin. So we made our way out the way we'd come in — fortunately, this time there were no people standing near that opening in the corridor.

Unlike *Voyager*, the *DS9* soundstage had a wide opening that you could fit a small plane through. Walking right in, we first noticed the Operations Center of the Space Station. A magnificent, two-and-a-half floor set, most of the consoles were covered with lime green tarps. Three people started walking through this set — maybe another V.I.P. tour — so we decided to walk past Ops to the station corridor set. Beyond the corridor were a couple of station crew quarters sets, complete with black velvet "space" outside the windows, and we snapped a few more pictures. We also got some nice ones of the corridor with cables spread all across the floor.

Unfortunately, we didn't get a chance to see the Promenade, as that was next door on Stage 17 (yes, Stages 4 and 17 were next to each other . . . I have no idea why). Indeed, I wouldn't see the

Promenade until three years later, when Lisa and I would sneak onto it the day before Paramount dismantled it forever. During that trip, I'd end up stealing a glass from Quark's Bar, but that's another story.

With little else left to look at, and with the other group having moved on, we decided to check out the Ops set. I took a few photos and was about to snap a shot of Lisa standing in the turbolift when I heard a voice from behind me.

"Excuse me, sir? Who are you with?" It was a security guard. I tried to think fast. Lisa beat me to it.

"We're supposed to meet with Tim Russ of *Voyager*," she tried to sound official.

"He's in a production meeting and told us we could look around," I said, and then I added with a friendly smile, ". . . as long as we didn't touch anything."

This entire time I'm thinking: *Please don't confiscate my camera! Oh, please don't confiscate my camera!*

The guard held up a clipboard, "I'm sorry, folks, but I can't let you stay here. *Voyager* is another show, and Mr. Russ doesn't work on this show."

I played dumb, "I thought they were both *Star Trek*."

"They are, but they're two separate shows. If you're with Mr. Russ, you can wait for him across the way on the *Voyager* stage. But I don't have you on my list, so I can't let you stay here. Sorry."

He didn't ask for my camera! "Oh, no problem," we answered. "We didn't know. We'll wait for him on the *Voyager* stage."

"Sorry again, folks. I just can't let you stay if you're not on my list."

We smiled and thanked him. He was so nice, and I'd half

expected to be mauled by attack dogs! We'd gotten two-and-a-half rolls of pictures of both *Star Trek* sets; I had nothing to complain about. Little did I know my day was just beginning.

Having now been "busted," Lisa and I decided it would be a good idea to try a little harder to hook up with Tim Russ. So we went back to his trailer and noticed that the door was now open. Knocking, we heard a "Come in" from inside. And there was Tim, on his cell phone, in full Tuvok make-up (ears and eyebrows), wearing his black uniform pants, no shirt, and a bathrobe and slippers. He motioned for us to come in and sit down.

Lisa and Tim had met before, so he recognized her. After he finished his call, he greeted us both and apologized for not being available earlier. Turns out he actually was in a production meeting (so I hadn't completely lied to that guard). He signed the contracts for Lisa and we chatted for a little as he asked Lisa how her trip to L.A. was going and who else she'd managed to sign up for the phone card promotion.

Then Tim had to head for another meeting, but he said they'd be filming starting around 2:15, and that we were welcome to stay and watch if we wanted. If we wanted?! As if he even needed to ask! He put on his blue-gray shirt and then his uniform jacket and walked us outside. Interestingly enough, he was still wearing slippers, and apparently wore them for most scenes except for those when his feet would be in the shot. So the next time you see Tuvok on *Voyager* and you can't see his feet, he's probably wearing slippers.

Realizing that we had an opportunity to take a picture not just with Tim Russ but with Tuvok himself in full makeup and uniform, we asked if he wouldn't mind posing for two shots. Two clicks of the shutter later and we were off for lunch in the

With Tim Russ outside his trailer. (Photo courtesy Jonathan Lane)

Paramount cafeteria. We were back at Stage 8 by two o'clock and headed inside. This time there were people all over the place, setting up for a bunch of scenes on the Bridge. No sooner had we rounded the corner from the soundstage entranceway when a man walked up to us. "Excuse me, can I help you?"

"We're here with Tim Russ," Lisa smiled.

"I'll have to check with Tim. Would you wait here?" He headed off in the other direction. Wow, what a difference three short hours made in security. We later found out this fellow was the technical director, and he returned about a minute later saying, "Okay, Tim says it's all right for you to be here. We'll be filming a few shots on the Bridge. I'll need you to stand over here, off to the side. The Captain doesn't like anyone she doesn't recognize to be in her line of sight when she's doing a scene."

"The Captain?" we thought. It turned out that everyone — cast, director, production crew — referred to Kate Mulgrew as "The Captain." Strange but true.

They were also quite serious about staying out of her line of sight. Once the scenes started filming, any time we edged up too close (to get a better view), someone would come over and shift us further back.

We stayed for about three hours watching them film what turned out to be just two scenes from the third season episode "The Swarm." One scene involved Kes coming onto the Bridge, warning that the Doctor's holographic matrix was degrading rapidly and asking for Harry Kim's help in Sickbay. The other scene had Janeway trying to communicate with the Swarm, followed by *Voyager* being hit by a polaron beam. When the beam hit, the ship was supposed to shake violently. To cue the actors when to react to the shaking, a production crew member would yell out "Jolt!" Everyone would then react as if the ship had been hit and the camera would be shaken slightly. We watched both scenes be filmed numerous times, with the word "Jolt!" being yelled out each time the second scene was shot. I found myself wondering: if it's illegal to yell "Fire!" in the middle of a crowded theater, would it also be illegal to yell "Jolt!" in the middle of a crowded starship?

When I saw the completed episode on television a couple of months later, these two scenes lasted only about two minutes (Kes' scene for 18 seconds, the other scene for one minute and 42 seconds). And watching them film, I understood why things take so long. There was a lot of preparation setting up the lighting and microphones, getting the characters' make-up fixed, making sure people were standing in the right places, and just having the actors deliver their lines correctly. While we waited for the scenes to be set up properly, some of the actors would kid around. At one point, feeling very silly, Robert Duncan McNeill (Tom Paris) and Garrett Wang (Harry Kim) hid under the helm console and started bobbing their heads up and down like prairie dogs.

While the scenes themselves were actively being shot, there were perhaps as many as 10 people standing all around the actors, especially "The Captain." It was as if they were swarming Kate Mulgrew, trying to get her autograph, except that no one got closer to her than about three feet, masterfully avoiding accidentally being seen in the shot. Lighting people, boom mike holders, make-up people, the director, the technical director, production assistants — all these people were grouped around the actors like a mob, but not one of them ever appeared on the final film. Just amazing! Even now, sometimes when I watch *Voyager* and other television shows, I try to imagine all of the people who were standing around these actors as they did their scenes, masterfully not getting into the shot.

We left a little after 5 p.m., thanking Tim Russ profusely. We never told him about our adventures wandering all over the sets and taking pictures. But looking back, it was quite an incredible (and lucky!) opportunity. Most people who get tours of the *Star Trek* sets aren't allowed to take pictures. Not only did we get pictures, we got pictures with us in them playing around while all the console lights were on and blinking. For two drooling *Star Trek* fans, this was truly a once-in-a-lifetime experience.

More Than Just Fans

Sometimes just watching a show or joining a fan club isn't enough; fans want to make their own mark on their favorite show. The following stories are written by people who started fan clubs, put up Web sites, wrote script treatments, and generally became more actively involved in the world of *Trek* than most fans do.

And here he is again, folks, Jonathan Lane! Who else can claim to be a professional Trekkie?!

Becoming a Professional Trekkie

BY JONATHAN LANE

Sometimes lightning does strike twice. At the end of 1993, I turned down an opportunity to work in the art department on *Star Trek* in order to concentrate on growing my multimedia (later Internet) development company here in Los Angeles. My Trekker friends thought I was nuts, turning down a once-in-a-lifetime chance to work on the show at Paramount Pictures, and perhaps I was. But less than three years later, that once-in-a-lifetime opportunity happened again, this time under slightly different circumstances, and I actually have that same company that pulled me away from a *Star Trek* job in the first place to thank for it.

2-Lane Media, which I founded in early 1993 with my brother David, started out creating interactive multimedia on CD-ROM and floppy disk. When Al Gore invented the Internet in 1995, 2-Lane Media branched out to making Web sites for clients that included Disney, Transamerica, Tenet Healthcare, and a CD-ROM game developer by the name of Interplay. In 1996, Interplay hired 2-Lane Media to create a Web site to help market their new *Star Trek: Starfleet Academy* CD-ROM game. The Web site needed to show elements from the game and be fun for *Trek* fans to navigate through. Naturally, 2-Lane's resident *Trek* expert (that's me) was brought in to manage the project.

The first thing we had to do was write a proposal for the client to submit to Paramount's licensing department, known as Viacom Consumer Products (or VCP). The concept was to create a virtual Starfleet Academy set in movie-era *Star Trek* time as an Internet site, with a section dedicated to training simulations (demos and screen captures from the game itself), a science lab (with game tips), the Commandant's office (where any contests/giveaways would be placed), and a cadet quarters area that would be filled with little "winks" to the hard core fans. These "winks" were trivia references that would mean little to "normal" people but would challenge any decent *Trek* fanatic to identify them all — a 3-D chess set, tribbles on the bed (more each time you visited the site), titles of books on the shelf, a Vulcan lyre hanging on the wall, a bust of Balok on the desk, a mirror showing the emblem of the *I.S.S. Enterprise*, a poster of the galaxy with a bird super-imposed, and much more. It was a lot of fun to plan out.

The challenge came in writing the actual proposal. I figured that Paramount was more likely to find people who knew licensing than people who knew both *Star Trek* and licensing. After all, by 1996, there were nearly 400 hours of filmed *Star Trek* episodes in existence. It was tough to know everything. Therefore, I proceeded from the assumption that whoever was going to be reading my proposal would likely be a "normal" person who wouldn't get most of my references unless I explained them.

And explain them I did . . . quite carefully. For example, in the cadet's quarters, there was a deck of playing cards which, when clicked, would show close-ups of certain of the cards. Part of the proposal went like this: "One of the cards will be the Jack of Hearts with Scotty's face on it. In the episode 'Wolf in the Fold,' Scotty was temporarily possessed by the spirit of Jack the Ripper, otherwise known as 'Redjac' or 'Red Jack.' Another card will be a black 7, but instead of spades or clubs, the suit will be black cats. The reason for this is in the episode 'Assignment: Earth,' the *Enterprise* crew met a man named Gary Seven (hence the '7') who had a mysterious black cat." And so it went, with careful and clear explanations of every "inside" *Trek* reference.

Although I hoped my extra time and effort would pay off with a quick approval of our proposal — and it did — what I did not expect was the call I received two days later from Juliet Dutton of Viacom Consumer Products. It seems that I had been correct in assuming VCP licensing people wouldn't know *Star Trek* inside and out. Indeed, Juliet had been at the job

A group of fans play dress-up at a convention (Photo courtesy Marc B. Lee)

seven months and was desperately trying to catch up on her episode watching, taking tapes home almost nightly. When she read my proposal, she called me up with a proposal of her own: "How would you like to be my personal *Star Trek* consultant?" Juliet was in charge of approving *Star Trek* CD-ROM games, and would typically get about one game script per month to review and provide guidance on. Not being a *Trek* expert, Juliet was finding it a rather daunting task to ensure that these games didn't violate the "sacred" continuity of the *Star Trek* franchise.

"What would I need to do?" I asked. "Well, I'd send you a

script every so often and you'd have about a week or so to read it. Then you could either write up your comments or tell them to me over the phone. We'd pay you $20 per hour." So she was saying that I'd get paid 20 bucks an hour to read about *Star Trek* and then talk about it on the telephone? I said yes.

Over the next few months, I read game scripts for a number of projects, including the epic *Klingon Academy* game from Interplay, the proposal for which was nearly 150 pages long! For most of the games, I would make comments like suggesting that Andorians be used instead of Tellarites for a particular scene, or that Troi would never say such-and-such a line. For one *DS9* game, the producers had completely misinterpreted the pah-wraiths, and on a *Voyager* game, the player gets promoted three or four times during the game while poor Harry Kim remains at the rank of Ensign for seven years! And all the while, I was billing hours, working from home at night and on the weekends, and actually able to legally deduct *Star Trek* purchases as business expenses on my tax returns!

Less than a year later, I began working with my second licensing person. This time, it wasn't CD-ROM games but rather the soon-to-open "*Star Trek: The Experience*" at the Las Vegas Hilton. Seems the nice folks who were constructing the attraction planned to have their own version of Quark's Bar and Restaurant and had chosen a diverse menu of drinks and food items. Unfortunately, their choices of names for these food and drink selections were, to put it gently, uninspired. Names like "galaxy burger" and "cosmic fries" were just not firing up the imaginations of the people at VCP. Kirsti, the VCP person in charge of this particular Paramount Parks attraction, was at a loss on how to handle this rather boring menu.

During a weekly staff meeting, Juliet suggested to Kirsti that she give me a call. "I've got this consultant I've been using, and he knows *Star Trek* backwards and forwards. He's pretty funny, too. Maybe he can write your menu."

The next thing I knew, I was holding two faxed lists of items, one for drinks, the other for food. I was given the ingredients of the drinks and general descriptions for the food items. Now it was my job to *Trek* 'em up!

Since the list of items was so long, I brought in some friends to help with the task — members of the *U.S.S. Angeles Star Trek* fan club here in L.A. During a Fourth of July barbeque, we sat around and came up with such winning food names as:

Isolinear Chips and Dips
The Holy Rings of Betazed (onion rings)
The Wrap of Khan
The Bacon Cheeseborger
The BBQ Continuum Pizza
Journey to Basil Pasta
Fisherman's Worf
The Pie of the Prophets (also known as Kai Pie)

Our drink names were equally inspired:

Tranya (of course)
Orion's Belt
The Vulcan Nerve Pinch
Risan Shine
Trill Chill
Wesley's Crush (the last three were part of the non-alcoholic drinks, known as "The Neutral Zone")

One of our drinks, the Warp Core Breach, actually made it into an episode of *Deep Space Nine* as a drink served at Quark's on the station.

Once the names were selected, I went to work writing up descriptions of every item. Here's a few examples of some of the food and drink descriptions:

> "The Pattern Buffer — This tasty drink simulates the effect of a transporter without the hassle of actually beaming anywhere."
> "The Red Shirt — A favorite drink of *Enterprise* security guards. It helps them pass the time while they're barricaded in their quarters trying to avoid landing party duty."
> "Shuttle Salad — A side salad to fill your hangar bay but not burst your cargo hold."
> "Tribble Tenders — Ever since Captain Sisko brought them back from the past, they've been over-running the kitchen, but they do taste just like chicken." (I'm surprised I got away with this one!)

An amusing story happened three and a half months later when I finally finished writing, rewriting, correcting, and perfecting the menu. It had finally been approved by Paramount and was ready to go to the printers barely a month before the attraction was to open to the public. It was now time to pay me. But the Las Vegas Hilton and Paramount Parks had forgotten to get my signature on a work-for-hire agreement, so I still had the rights to what I'd written.

Now, I knew they were planning to sell the menu in the gift shop as a keepsake, and maybe I could get some of the royalties from it. Of course, that was the last thing in the world that the Las Vegas Hilton wanted to have happen, but I could have forced the point, since it was too late to get someone to rewrite the menu in time. I was stuck in a dilemma. Should I try to get some royalties or just be a good little Trekkie and sign their agreement? I asked Juliet and Kirsti what they thought.

"Well, you certainly could make an issue out of it, but that wouldn't make you all that popular around here," they told me. "Right now, the people at VCP are very impressed with the menu, and you'll likely get more work from us in the future. If you do get any royalties, they'll likely be about 25 cents per menu. You'll probably make a lot more money staying on everyone's good side and just signing the agreement. But it's your choice."

They were right, of course, and I decided to sign the work-for-hire contract and submit my invoice. And do you want to hear the punchline? They ended up putting a price tag of $10 each for the food and drink menus separately, which was outrageously high. In the first six months that the "*Star Trek: The Experience*" was open, only a handful of menus sold, but several thousand were stolen by restaurant customers! (I stole one myself!) And I did go on to make lots more money from VCP than I would have ever made from royalties on those overpriced menus.

After the menu, I was handed around the VCP offices like a plate of cookies. I worked with numerous other licensees. I worked with a European company that was creating a traveling science exhibit that would use *Star Trek* to illustrate science and technology concepts. I worked with Sound Source

Interactive writing over 800 trivia questions for their *Star Trek: The Game Show* CD-ROM game, hosted by Q. (I had suggested they call it *Star Trek: Q and A*, but they didn't.) And I worked for over a year and a half with CyberAction, which created a series of digital *Star Trek* trading cards for computers (complete with video clips, sound bytes, trivia questions, and lots of surprises). Before CyberAction went out of business in 2001, I wrote the text for hundreds of digital trading cards covering the first four TV series and the nine motion pictures, as well as lots of background info.

Did I ever meet any famous *Trek* actors doing the consultant gig? A few, but not too many. Since the job did involve driving to Paramount every so often, I'd usually combine my visits to the VCP offices with a leisurely stroll around the Paramount lot. Somehow, I'd always wind up around the *Star Trek* soundstages, and sometimes the actors would be hanging out, usually in costume. I saw Robert Beltran, Tim Russ, and Robert Picardo a few times. And once I saw Marc Alaimo in his Gul Dukat make-up and wearing a T-shirt. It was weird seeing his Cardassian neck flapping up and down like Jello over his shirt!

Surely the highlight of working with licensees came during the making of the aforementioned *Star Trek: The Game Show* CD-ROM. John DeLancie played Q, quizzing contestants (the players), whom he had kidnapped from the Alpha Quadrant, about the history of the Federation, Klingon and Romulan Empires, etc. All the questions had to be written as if *Star Trek* really existed (i.e. no episode titles or questions about the actors or producers).

The problem for John was reading hundreds of questions containing names and words that were tongue-twisters on the

John DeLancie charms fans at FEDCON 7. (Photo courtesy Susanne Dörfler)

best of days. I had to sit in the sound booth with him for nearly seven hours, reading each question first and pronouncing the names correctly, after which he would read the question himself as Q. During breaks we chatted about his career, how he brings the characters that he plays to life beyond what's written in the script, and his feelings about the various *Star Trek* series. (He wasn't particularly thrilled with *Voyager* nor with most of its cast, aside from Robert Picardo — Jeri Ryan hadn't yet joined the series.)

Most recently, I wrote a *Star Trek* reference book called

Starship Spotter. Brought in at the last minute, my friend Alex Rosenzweig and I put together backgrounds and specifications for 30 spaceships from all of the *Star Trek* series. Images were created by another of my friends, Adam "Mojo" Lebowitz, and generated on the computer from actual digital 3-D models used on the show. With less than a month until deadline, their writer had abandoned the project, and Alex and I were forced to write 45 pages of text in a mere 18 days! Fortunately, since I'd worked so extensively already with VCP, I was able to talk directly to the fellow who would be checking over my facts for the book. Indeed, he would likely have handed the text off to me to double-check anyway, so having me write it in the first place saved us a step. And that's how I was able to write a book in less than three weeks.

All in all, it's been a wild and wacky trip. And while it sounds like mainly fun and games, there was actually a lot of hard work required. Countless hours were spent watching and re-watching episodes, taking copious notes and marking down time codes, reading through very technical game descriptions, and staying up to all hours writing trivia questions and trading cards and book chapters and menus — always trying to beat a deadline. And I had to do this while I had a regular job to go to during business hours that had nothing to do with *Star Trek*. But the rewards have been more than satisfying, especially to a hard-core Trekker like me. I've left my small mark on the history of *Star Trek*. Although my Las Vegas menu has been changed a couple of times (it's not nearly as funny anymore, ahem), the original is still for sale. *Starship Spotter* marks my first-ever professionally published book, and I'm helping Mojo with his next one, *Unseen Frontier*. And although I don't get called quite as often to consult for VCP anymore, I still drive over to the Paramount lot every so often to "do lunch" with my licensing friends and stroll past the *Trek* soundstages.

So, yes, sometimes lightning does strike twice. And combined with a little faith, some luck, perseverance, and a lot of hard work, I've realized my dream of becoming a professional Trekkie.

There are many stories of fans who try to help out a celebrity, completely unbeknownst to that person. Kathy Warren has been working tirelessly to promote Brent Spiner's CD — here's hoping that maybe he reads this piece and finds out about it.

Lending a Hand to Ol' Yellow Eyes

BY KATHY WARREN

I'm a born-again Trekker. When I was a teenager, back in the '60s, I was an avid fan of *The Original Series*; I even made a little delta shield to wear to high school. I saw every *TOS* movie as soon as it came out, except the second one (I refused to see Spock die until I was sure he would live again in the next movie).

When *Star Trek: The Next Generation* debuted, I took one look at the weird crew, ugly uniforms, and goofy-looking ship and swore never to watch it. I think the biggest problem I had with *TNG* was that I assumed they were telling us that all the old guys were dead. (Little did I know!) Then a few weeks after "All Good Things" aired, a blurb in the *TV Guide* caught my eye. It said, "Data's shuttlecraft explodes . . ." Those three words changed my life. "How can they do that?" I gasped. "They can't kill him, he's a regular!" I watched that episode, "The Most Toys," and immediately became hooked by the show and the character of Data.

I began watching every night from that night on, kicking myself for not having watched from the beginning. The more I watched, the more I loved Data and the more impressed I became with the incredible actor who brings him to life, Brent Spiner.

In January of 1995, I attended my second *Star Trek* convention and purchased Brent's CD, *Ol' Yellow Eyes Is Back*. I remember playing it for the first time on my roommate's boom box while I took the Christmas tree down. With every song, I became more impressed with his awesome vocal talent and incredibly sexy style. I told my roommate, who was equally impressed, "This record doesn't need to be the best-kept secret of the *Trek* set, it needs to go mainstream!" Being a former professional singer myself, I can't stand to see great vocal talent go unrecognized and not rewarded, so I made up my mind to try to get it some air time.

I called our local Big Band radio station, WAMB, and they told me to come up with the CD on a Sunday afternoon when the program director, Ken Bramming, was doing a ball game broadcast. Before making the trip to the station, I called the record's producer and asked if they would mind if I tried to get it played on some radio stations. The producer's wife said sure, why not. So *Project Ol' Yellow Eyes* was born.

That Sunday, a friend and I drove to Nashville and met with Mr. Bramming. He loved the CD and agreed to play it on the

Ol' Yellow Eyes himself — Brent Spiner — shows off his singing voice with Marina Sirtis at FEDCON 8. (Photo courtesy Susanne Dörfler)

air. He even did a "Name the Mystery Singer" contest. His praise for the CD encouraged me to contact more radio stations. My experience working with a grassroots political organization had taught me that a few people, or even one person, can accomplish a great deal, so I obtained a list of big band format radio stations and started calling.

I used the curiosity approach, telling the program directors that I was engaged in a personal project of promoting an album of well-known standards sung by a very popular performer. I offered to send them a tape with two of the selections from the album and told them if they liked what they heard, I would contact the producers and they would send the station a CD to play on the air. Because of the, shall we say, *checkered* history of albums by *Star Trek* stars, I wouldn't tell them who they would be listening to. I wanted them to listen without prejudice or preconceived notions of what it would sound like. With only a couple of exceptions, they accepted the offer of the tape. Usually, the only ones who refused to listen to it were the ones who pried it out of me who the artist was. Their loss.

After roughly a week and a half, I would call them back and ask if they'd gotten the tape and had a chance to listen to it. Approximately 85% of the program directors loved the selections, "Embraceable You" and "Zing! Went the Strings of My Heart," and asked for a copy of the CD. And they were amazed when I told them they had been listening to Brent Spiner from *Star Trek: The Next Generation*. One gentleman raved that he was better than Tony Bennett. Another asked where this album had been all these years. I spoke to the receptionist at a station in West Virginia and when I told her who the singer was she told me her boss was a big *Star Trek* fan. When the program director came on the phone and asked me whose music she had been listening to, I asked her, "Does the name 'Data' mean anything to you?" After a few seconds of stunned silence, she shouted, "Oh, my God!" and told me how much she loved it.

It was an incredibly gratifying experience to share Brent's music with these people who were able to introduce it to millions of listeners in this country and in Europe. A couple of gentlemen

"What?! My album's gone to number one?!" Brent Spiner goofs around on stage. (Photo courtesy Susanne Dörfler)

who produced syndicated shows broadcast in several European cities as well as America took the CD and included it in their shows. It was especially rewarding to hear all of these radio professionals praise Brent's voice, style, and choice of material. Most of them asked me when he was going to record another CD. I wish I could have told them they, and we, would have more of this beautiful music soon. Brent always jokes that when *Ol' Yellow Eyes* broke even and started making money, he would do another album. Well, Brent, I helped make that happen for you. Now I hope some day you'll be able to keep your end of the bargain.

This project was only one of the ways *Star Trek* fandom has had a positive effect on my life. In addition to taking up writing again, thanks to the inspiration these characters provide, I have made very good friends I wouldn't have met if not for *Star Trek*. I have always believed *Star Trek* had a positive influence on people's lives because it shows a very positive view of the future that awaits mankind if we can get our act together and actually learn to live together without destroying this beautiful planet and ourselves. It extols the highest virtues of humanity and shows us, in a very entertaining fashion, where we can use some serious improvement. But aside from its positive vision and social conscience, it's just plain fun.

Voyager's Delights

BY DANIELLE RUDDY

www.voyagersdelights.com

This year marks *Star Trek*'s 35th anniversary; *Star Trek* aired its first episode on September 8, 1966. Since then we have had four spin-offs from the original series including *Star Trek: The Next Generation*, *Deep Space Nine*, *Voyager*, and now a new series entitled *Enterprise*. Aside from the five TV series, the animated series, and the films, a *Star Trek* fan has a lot to enjoy.

I started to watch *Star Trek* in reruns in 1984, when I was about seven years old. My father was the one who had gotten me into *Star Trek*. At the time, my father worked for Zenith installing televisions for hotels and hospitals. One day he was working at a hotel in Cambridge, Massachusetts. He had just arrived at the job site and was stepping out of his van when two men attacked him in the hotel's parking garage. They broke his ribs, held a screwdriver up to his neck, and stole his wallet, his van, and the televisions that he was bringing to install in the hotel. He came home that night from the hospital.

Of course he wasn't well at all and he couldn't sleep. So I told my father that I wasn't feeling well (a little white lie just so I could stay up with him). We watched *M*A*S*H* and then he flipped the TV station on *Star Trek*. I instantly fell in love with the show. I remember telling him that he couldn't put *M*A*S*H* back on until *Star Trek* was over.

Ever since then every night I would tune in, to go on another adventure with Captain Kirk and company. I must have seen those episodes at least a thousand times each before *TNG* came out in 1987. I remember hating the pilot episode, but something kept me tuning in every week and I found myself enjoying the show more and more. *TNG* captured some of the essence of *TOS*. I love the moral dilemmas that make you stop and think and I agree with Federation principles.

Then in 1993 *DS9* came along and, like with *TNG*, I watched the first episode and really didn't like it at all. I didn't watch it again until season seven, and the only reason I did was to see what was going on in the Federation in case *Voyager* got home. But this time, I found myself being drawn into it.

Voyager was next, making its debut in 1995. Once again I found myself drawn into the *Star Trek* world. I loved the Janeway character. As a 24-year-old woman I find her character a source of strength and a wonderful role model. It was nice to see women finally being treated as equals.

Voyager also inspired me to create a Web site, *Voyager's*

Robert Duncan McNeill laughs with fans at a convention. (Photo courtesy Susanne Dörfler)

Delights, back in 1999 and it is still running strong. At the time I barely even knew how to turn on the computer. So in a way *Star Trek* made me learn how to use a computer and how to design a Web site and create *Star Trek* music videos. Also in a way I owe my job to *Star Trek*. Today I'm working as a store manager at a small printing company and part of my job includes typesetting and design work on the computer.

The fifth series, *Enterprise*, once again has me falling in love with *Star Trek*. I enjoy the show immensely and I look forward to my Wednesday nights with the crew of the *Enterprise*.

Gene Roddenberry's vision has touched thousands if not millions of lives (myself included) across the world. He provided us with a glimpse of the future and a vision of peace and prosperity; one where mankind didn't fight over land and money, where there was no hunger, and it didn't matter what color, race, or gender you were — you were treated as equals. I can only hope that one day *Star Trek* — a work of fiction — will become a reality.

May *Star Trek* live long and prosper for years and years to come.

This is a great story about becoming president of the fan club for Chase "Leeta" Masterson.

A Boy and His Twig Phaser Are Not Easily Parted

BY GEORGE "STOMPY" KUHR, PRESIDENT, THE OFFICIAL CHASE MASTERSON FAN CLUB

I have been a *Star Trek* fan for a very long time. As a young child growing up in Canada I was able to watch *The Original Series* in the early afternoon in 1966 and 1967. Canada had a rule at the time that in order for American television to be broadcast on Canadian channels we had to get it first. Don't ask me who came up with the rules; all I do know is that *Star Trek* aired while I was at my babysitter's house and before my mom got home from work, and I was able to see the Gorn and the Klingons and the phaser fights well before my bedtime.

We played *Star Trek* in the backyard: a tool shed was the *Enterprise*, a book of matches and a glued-on button was the communicator, and a twig turned around backwards was a phaser (even at three years old we knew that the handles for the phasers were in the front — we were smart kids).

As I grew older I became aware of a larger body of *Star Trek* fans. After the show was off the air, fans began to get together at conventions. In 1976 I attended my first con and was hooked for life. During that time in my life I didn't have a lot of friends, but I did have a very active imagination. I used to act out scenes from *Star Trek*; I'd carry my model communicator with me to talk to the ship while I was on a "landing party" mission. I used to dream about mailing myself in a big box to the *Star Trek* sets or that maybe one of the actors would come over to my house for dinner.

In the late '70s we saw the popularity of *Star Trek* and sci-fi flourish. We saw *Star Trek* emerge on the big screen and our heroes come back to life. We moved into the '80s and saw Gene catch lightning in a bottle again with the advent of *TNG*. *Star Trek* was indeed alive and well and continued with *DS9* and *Voyager*.

Today there are countless books, CDs, games, a new series on UPN, and just about anything else you can imagine. *Star Trek* has touched every facet of my life. I carry a *Star Trek* credit card, I have *Star Trek* checks, my son is named "Scotty" — heck I even got my job because of *Star Trek*, but that's a whole 'nother story.

I write this so that you'll understand just how much this

club means to me. For me, to be allowed to belong to a great group of people, to be part of *Star Trek* in some small way, is a validation of everything I've been doing my whole life. It is an affirmation of the little kid fighting a Gorn on Cetus III with a stick, to a grown-up man writing a story on a computer and sending it at the speed of light to someone halfway across the country so that you can read it.

I had been involved in *Star Trek* fandom for many years but never very actively until the Internet came along. I was able to communicate with people all over the world, to share ideas and help in ways I never could before. The president of Chase's club needed a new Webmaster so I volunteered for the job. The first

Chase Masterson with George "Stompy" Kuhr. (Photo courtesy George Kuhr)

time I met Chase she took me out to dinner and stole David "Darth Vader" Prowse's French fries and gave them to me. As the club grew and changed, there were several people who took on the role of club president, but luckily I was still the Webmaster. When the former president stepped down I asked if I could take on the job since I was doing a lot of the online role anyway. Chase agreed and I was in.

On September 8, 2001, the 35th anniversary of the debut of *Star Trek*, I had the great honor of hosting Chase Masterson in my home. Chase was in town for a whirlwind convention tour that took her from L.A. to New York to Dallas to Phoenix and back to L.A. all within 48 hours. I was able to pick up Chase from the airport and work the show with her while she was here in town. (I am still enough of a geeky Trekkie that I get excited at this sort of thing.) The fact that one of the stars of *Star Trek* actually came to my home was an *enormous* thrill for me. Is Chase just a person? Yeah. Is she just an actress doing a job? Yeah. Was she just a person who needed a ride from the airport? Yeah. But to me she is also the culmination of 35 years of trying to fit in, of wanting to have a family to belong to, of being part of a group of my heroes who I looked up to and admired and modeled my whole life on. To have your life affirmed in that manner doesn't happen too often for a person. For me, to have it occur on the 35th Anniversary of the show is just an incredible experience.

Thank you Chase for making the dreams of a little boy come true.

As I was driving Chase to the convention I had forgotten that the Dallas Cowboys were having their season opener the same day. We drove headlong into the fray. I quickly ran out of

Chase shows off her steamy side on an Alaskan Star Trek cruise in 1998 as she serenades a fan. (Photo courtesy Mark A. Cafurello)

gas and chugged into a station to fill up while Chase did acrobatics in the front seat to get ready for the show. I came up with an alternate plan to skirt the traffic; the only problem is I had no idea where the alternative route would end up. After driving for a bit I came upon a route I vaguely knew and got back on track. I got Chase to the convention in plenty of time to set up. I escorted her in the front door and through the throng of Trekkers waiting to get in. I heard whispers of, "Hey, that's Leeta!" and other startled gasps from the fans. We got things set up and the show was on. During the course of the day I was able to chat with Stuart Moss from the original series as well as

BarBara Luna who signed a picture I had taken with her several months before (she signed it "To Stompy, from your biggest fan, BarBara Luna"). I also spoke with Larry Montaigne who had been originally slated to play Spock and was on a couple of *TOS* episodes.

Perhaps the greatest thrill, aside from having Chase at my place, was to speak with Michael Forrest, who played Apollo. We chatted about Leslie Parrish, his co-star on *Star Trek*, and some of his non-*Trek* roles that I had seen him in. What a gracious and incredible man. I must admit at being totally taken aback when he stood up to take a picture with me. I'm 5'7" and he is a *really* tall man.

I had a great time over the course of the weekend. It is not often that a person gets to live their lifelong dream. I have Chase to thank for that and the members of her club for allowing me to be part of the whole *Star Trek* Universe. Inside me there is a three-year-old boy running up and down green hills with a twig for a phaser, and once in a while he gets to peek out and tell me he's still alive. May Gene Roddenberry's dream stay alive in all of us.

Making My Mark

BY JEANNA F. GALLO

I've been a *Trek* fan since the first episode of the original series aired. As a child, I was among the phalanx of fans who wrote NBC back then to protest the premature cancellation of the show. I was skeptical of any attempt to go home again with *Star Trek: The Next Generation*, but Roddenberry's vision, embodied in Patrick Stewart, Brent Spiner, Gates McFadden, Marina Sirtis, Michael Dorn, LeVar Burton, Jonathan Frakes, and their characters won me over until it became the best adult sci-fi I've ever seen on television. I began to dabble in writing some fan-fic for the old paper 'zines and then began writing to the producers to thank them for making such an intelligent series.

This production team was noted for inviting and listening to the ideas of the fans. They even allowed would-be scriptwriters to submit a script without an agent and to make "pitches." I struck up a correspondence and friendship with executive producer, Jeri Taylor, which lasts to this day. I sent her some material, one of which evolved into the atypical episode "Sub Rosa,"

Gates McFadden
(Photo courtesy Marc B. Lee)

which was intended as a bouquet for the lovely Dr. Beverly Crusher. They got my mind's-eye view of the Scots planetary colony exactly right. I also requested that Brannon Braga write the episode (Jeri did the story) and that Jon Frakes would direct it and I got my wish list. I have a tiny credit in the closing; if you blink you'll miss it. But I'm also credited on the title page of the script, which really blew me away. Especially when Jeri thoughtfully sent me a copy warmly autographed by her, Braga, Gates, and Frakes. My favorite *Trek* collectible of all time.

When *Voyager* was in production, Jeri sent me the series' "bible" and I was invited to submit concepts. One of these was turned into "Distant Origin" about evolved dinosaurs from earth, an idea I had been trying to interest them in since *Next Generation* (I did not receive credit for this one due to a change in studio policy).

This series really helped to keep my chin up during a rough time in my life as *Trek*, at its best, presents an optimistic view of the future. It's rare to see producers who actually care about what the fans thought of their show and who attempt to incorporate concepts put forward by fans. They gave a lot of self-confidence and allowed a lifelong sci-fi fan and Trekker to make her tiny mark on *Trek* history. Thank you, Jeri!

A Voyage Inside Paramount with a Very Incompetent Person

BY BULENT HASAN

I've watched *Star Trek* all my life. One of my first memories was seeing *Star Trek* in the theaters when it was first released.

Slowly, I got into the whole *Next Generation* shows, and soon afterwards, I got heavily into *Voyager*. I always dreamed about being behind the scenes.

In August 2000 that happened. I had been given a consulting contract with Paramount Studios and was also given a tour of the Lot. Since we had V.I.P. passes, we got to have the tour in one of those extended golf carts that seat nine comfortably! The problem was, our tour guide knew *squat* about film, film history, or the *Star Trek* franchise. Since *Star Trek* has had a long history at the Lot, one would assume she'd know something about at least how it got put together, which film/show was filmed here, but no. She kept making references to *The Brady Bunch* and *I Love Lucy*. The *I Love Lucy* spiel was informative, but my problem was that we were given a tour by a newbie who only read a pamphlet and had no previous experience with film! I convinced her that showing us anything to do with *Star Trek* would be all right with the Lot considering we are on a V.I.P. tour. Slowly but surely, we got to see something *Star Trek*-related.

The Gower theater on the Lot was 'refurbished' by the art department, and it was for an episode of *Voyager*, the one where Tom Paris does a holodeck recreation of a 1950s-style movie theater for a date with B'Elanna. Also, we got onto Stage 16, where *Star Trek* has a satellite set. It's where they built the sets for the alien ships and there was a large mountainside with a cave for filming (it's been in tons of episodes, but add a rock here, change the lighting there and it's different every time). Then, far off in the corner sat the Delta Flyer. Just the interior set sat there. I didn't know what it was until I walked towards it and noticed the "windshield" design that the Delta Flyer is famous for. I stepped inside and took as many pictures as I possibly could. Also, Borg set pieces were hanging from the ceiling of the studio by chains.

As we drove around a bit more in the golf cart we stopped to see a kiosk with some pictures. I noticed the parking lot had a strange three-foot-tall concrete wall built around it, and to one side (beside the water tower) was a 100 x 70-foot-tall wall with clouds painted on it. Then I said out loud, "They filmed *Star Trek IV* here!" The tour guide had no idea what I was talking about.

I went on and told everybody in the cart that they used this area as a pool years ago in the '50s and covered it up to be used as a parking lot. For *Star Trek IV* they dug it 15 to 20 feet down into the ground and it was filled up with water. At the end of the film the front of the Klingon Bird of Prey was sticking out of the top of the water, along with the animatronic whale back and tail. The people in the cart, along with the tour guide, never knew this.

Then off to Vegas, where I saw Tom Jones perform. He ended his show and started to bow to the audience, and I quickly pulled my camera out and took a quick snapshot. When I returned home, it turns out that as I had pulled out my camera, I had pushed out one roll of film. That roll of film had the pictures of the Delta Flyer on it.

I can now only tell this story. The entire roll of film was ruined, and even the Tom Jones photos weren't that great. Although, it turns out that one photo of Tom Jones that I took is when he turned to bow at his band, and his butt is in the frame. For me, that photo kind of sums up what I thought of the Paramount lot V.I.P. tour!

When I was contacting various fan club presidents to see if they'd be interested in writing stories about how they first met the Trek *star and began working with him or her, I received a funny note back from the president of the Tim Russ fan club that said, "I think it would be a little strange for me to do that, since he's my brother." We chatted back and forth and then she offered to write a story anyway, from the perspective of a family member who is working with her brother to reach out to* Trek *fans:*

Tuvok, My Brother

BY ANGELA RUSS

I have always been close to both of my brothers. We have traveled together for as long as I can remember, and when Tim landed his role on *Star Trek: Voyager*, no one was happier for him than I was. After all, he had landed a good paying job for the next seven years.

I became a fan by default, joining millions of others who watched the series. But, the idea of Tim working with someone he didn't know to form a fan club turned my stomach. He did not necessarily have the patience of Tuvok, and was not comfortable expressing his feelings in front of a perfect stranger. He is very sociable, but is better one-on-one than in a crowded setting. Like Tuvok, he is very logical and extremely intelligent. However, what Tuvok lacks in humor, Tim makes up for 10 times over. There was also the issue of trust. Would he have to watch everything he said in front of this person? Would his

Tim Russ with his sister Angela at FEDCON 6. (Photo courtesy Susanne Dörfler)

seven-year *Star Trek* experience eventually be in some unauthorized book somewhere? An actor can't just randomly pick someone to oversee his or her fan club, fan mail, or Web site. Personalities have to mesh, and whoever is close has access to personal information, as well as an actor's person.

From day one, Tim was being bombarded with requests, but wanted to have control over what was going on. I was the logical choice, but my brother, Michael, partnered with me to travel from one convention to another (see page 123). We started with an Official Fan Club, with paid membership, which disbanded in April 2000. It consisted of an autographed photo, several newsletters a year, and postcard notices to fans about his appearances.

I also process his fan mail so he can get through it within a reasonable amount of time. I attend conventions with him for the purpose of schlepping and selling his photos and other merchandise for donations to his charities. We donate everything from cash and auction collectibles, to the hotel toiletries we have left over from a trip, to the wearable items given to Tim. I recommend themes and assist Tim with on-stage entertainment for his conventions when he needs help. And, finally, I am here for any support he needs — emotionally or professionally — just as he is for me.

I must say that I found *Star Trek* fans to be some of the most patient fans I have ever encountered. They put up with delayed newsletters, endless lines, and over-crowded conventions without public complaint. Tim recognizes that there are millions of closet fans, in other words, the people who don't attend cons. When he is recognized, he speaks with fans graciously, and moves on. His fans are doctors, lawyers, engineers, kids — all races, creeds, colors, and ages. Tim is easily recognized around the world.

The fans are the reason Tim had a paycheck. He never loses sight of that, and he never wants to disappoint them, which is one of the reasons he came up with fan participation skits, song parodies, and independently produced music CDs for his conventions. The *Star Trek: Voyager* run has been a pleasure to behold and a wonderful experience to share with my brother and the family. I'm honored to have had the opportunity to assist him through it.

The Continuing Adventures of the Starship Secondprize

BY ALAN DECKER

I first started watching *The Original Series* back in 1986 when I was 12 years old, and I would say that it shaped my moral view and my dealings with others to an extent (either that or it perfectly meshed with the values my parents had already given me. I'd say six of one, half dozen of the other). I wouldn't say that *Star Trek* changed my life, though, until 1992. That October, while I was a freshman in college, I began writing a comedic story set in the *Trek* universe about the crew of the Starship Secondprize after a lunch conversation with a good friend. My friends read it, they laughed at the jokes and the characters (many of whom shared personality traits with my friends), and that was to be the end of it.

Until a couple months later, when I wrote another one.

It's now nine years later. The comedy series, *Star Traks*, has its own Web site consisting of the original stories plus five spin-offs written by myself and three other writers. I've met many people through the site, a few of whom have become very dear friends. One woman who enjoyed *Traks* began writing me from Vancouver, B.C. We became close enough friends that she flew from Vancouver to Baton Rouge, Louisiana, where my wife and I lived at the time, just to visit. None of these friendships would have existed without *Traks.*

The point where I truly realized just how far the stories were reaching came just after my son was born. Being a proud papa, I posted the announcement of his birth on my Web site. Soon thereafter, I received e-mails from as far away as France, India, and Australia congratulating me.

In the end, I owe all of this fun to *Star Trek*, and I'm sure many fan-fic writers have stories similar to mine. Part of the power of *Star Trek* is the community it has created around the world. Whether we meet through conventions, online discussion groups, or just because we e-mailed someone who wrote a *Trek* fan-fic story we liked, our interest in *Trek* gives us the common ground on which we can build deeper, lasting friendships.

I approached Joyce after seeing her in the Trekkies *documentary, and she was very kind, and generously wrote this wonderful piece about what it was like to work with William Shatner.*

The William Shatner Connection

BY JOYCE MASON, WILLIAM SHATNER OFFICIAL FAN CLUB PRESIDENT

I have lived and worked in New York all my life. I spent 23 years working on Wall Street for a very large, prestigious law firm. The last thing in the world I ever expected was to run a fan club, much less a fan club for a world-famous actor like William Shatner.

Nevertheless, changes happen when we least expect them and the changes in my very settled life began in 1981 when my sister, Gloria, became quite ill. It was one of those undiagnosed diseases, the kind that completely stumps the doctors. It took four long years before we discovered it was cancer, but by then it was far too late. Those were the hardest four years of my entire life. Part of the manifestation of the disease was a completely unpredictable and overwhelming mental and emotional reaction that was a constant cause of intense worry. I was living with her and never knew what I would find when I came home or what might happen at night. The one and only bright spot during that horrendous period was *Star Trek: TOS*. The show came on at midnight Monday through Friday and oh, how I cherished that one hour. It kept me going. I would lose myself in the stories, never tiring of them or getting bored of the repeats. I just kept on loving them and looking forward to them every night. It helped me to survive. Then on January 5, 1985, only two weeks after her diagnosis, Gloria died and I grieved deeply and felt lost. My attention had been so centered on Gloria that little else had been going on in my life during that time. What was I to do now? For four years my life was predictable, now it wasn't.

A friend sent me an application to join a fan club, the William Shatner Fellowship. I thought it was a joke. After all, no one joined fan clubs except teenagers. What did I know? I had never attended a convention; I had never even seen the *Star Trek* movies because I couldn't leave my sister alone, no matter how badly I wanted to go. In any event, I joined just to see what it was like. When I received the first newsletter, I was surprised to read an article about a William Shatner Weekend, a weekend in which the actor joined with the fans for several visits. That sounded like a blast, but I still decided not to go figuring I was too old and too sophisticated. My best friend convinced me that I should stop with the excuses and just go. After all, I had a lot of vacation time and no plans. I hadn't been to Los Angeles before so I could always cut out and go sightseeing. So I decided to go, but just to be on the safe side, I booked

Joyce Mason with William Shatner in April 1999. (Photo by Jane Singer, courtesy Joyce Mason)

a tour up the coast to San Francisco where I would spend several days exploring the city.

I paid my fee and arranged to attend the weekend. The first night was a get-together cocktail party. Being from New York, I dressed for a cocktail party, pearls and all. Everyone was in jeans. I remember standing in the back of the room trying, surreptitiously, to remove my pearls when I spotted another overdressed, embarrassed, wish-I-could-disappear duplicate of myself. I made a beeline for my fellow sufferer. Her name was Annie and she was from Seattle, Washington. Annie was the director of the video educational department for the state of Washington. We hit it off like two ducks sharing an umbrella and have been close friends ever since.

Bill signs autographs for his fans at a Shatner Weekend, 1996. (Photo courtesy Joyce Mason)

Helen Molloy, the president of the William Shatner Fellowship, came over to introduce herself. She also worked for a law firm, so was delighted to meet another "victim" of the law firm syndrome, to have someone with whom to compare adventures and misadventures.

The entire weekend was incredible: no teenagers, all adults, all fans, all really nice people, even if they did wear jeans. And, Bill Shatner did indeed show up, time after time. We met him for the first time on Saturday when he rode his horse for us, then again on Saturday evening when he showed up for our banquet. He came around to every table to say hello (something he still does at every "Shatnered Weekend"). He was so gracious, with a kind word or lighthearted comment for each fan. I later found out he dreaded the dinner. Every time he looked up from his food he found 110 pairs of eyes staring at him. He was certain that every time he opened his mouth to take a bite, he would dribble it down his chin, all over his shirt.

By the time the weekend was over and it was time to leave, I felt I was leaving friends I had known all my life. We had sat up all night like silly kids, just sharing and enjoying. After such a long time of pain it was what I needed to feel alive again and I treasured it. The trip to San Francisco was pleasant enough, but a bore by comparison to L.A.

The following November my firm opened an office in Los Angeles and the opportunity for me to move there as Office Manager was mine if I wanted it. I immediately accepted and on January 5, 1986, one year to the day since the death of my sister, I landed in Los Angeles and began a new and completely different life.

Helen and I became close friends and I was delighted to help her with the club as much as possible. I started writing articles for the newsletter and, eventually, much to my own surprise, I was asked to help with the interviews. Frankly, it was nothing short of a miracle that I survived the first one. Helen asked me to meet her for an interview with Bill at the Equestrian Center in Burbank. My job was to observe Helen doing an actual interview. When I arrived Helen announced she had forgotten her tape recorder and left to get it. A minute or so later Bill arrived and asked if we could start the interview. I told him Helen would be back soon but he didn't want to wait. He felt we could handle it. I had no notes, no preparation, no tape recorder, and no choice. So, I dutifully followed Bill into the barn's office and went to clear a table for some papers and photos I had for him to sign. Simultaneously, Bill bent to clear the same table and — WHACK! Our heads met midway over the table, the papers dropped on the floor, glasses went flying and I prayed I would die. Muttering all kinds of weak, whimpering apologies, I cautiously bent with Bill to pick up the debris and pretended like nothing had happened. The interview is, to this day, a blur but I did get something. (I must have because I printed it, but so help me, I have no memory of how it happened.) Maybe he just dictated to me, recognizing a pathetic idiot when he saw one. In any event, it was a discouraging beginning.

Helen retired several years later and Bill asked me if I would take over the club. I was hesitant but, let's face it, you just don't say no to William Shatner. Thus began 10 years of a tremendous amount of work combined with excitement, headaches, and a lot of fun.

Eventually I was contacted by one of the club members, who was also a Webmaster. He offered to develop a Web site for the club. Robert and I clicked perfectly. We spent hours on the phone developing ideas and making plans. I continued to write and Robert did the programming. The result of that was an ambitious, fun-filled, and beautiful site. We were very proud of it and felt it reflected the Shatner persona perfectly.

The interviews with Bill were always unpredictable and usually a lot of fun. He is most atypical in just about everything. At one interview, I had to meet him at the barn again (Bill loves the barn) along with a French reporter and her photographer. Bill hates to have his picture taken, but he understands the necessity for them and is quite gentlemanly about it. This photographer, however, was being a bit more than pushy. Although he had taken numerous photos already, he wanted Bill to pose with a horse but Bill didn't have a horse of his own in this particular stable. However, not to be deterred by minor obstacles, Bill simply walked into one of the barns, picked a horse, put a halter on it, and prepared to bring it out. Legal or not, the French reporter, whose English left something to be desired, had followed Bill into the barn. She was obviously not used to horses and when the animal backed up she became terrified and found herself pinned, spread eagle, at the back of the stall. The expression on her face was one of horror but Bill quickly came to her rescue, getting both the reporter and the horse out safely. However, when the photographer turned his back to Bill to prepare for yet another shot, the five-year-old that is usually just under Bill Shatner's skin pushed his way to the top and like a kid he stuck his tongue out at the photographer, which quickly turned back into a completely engaging smile when the pesky man turned back. Watching the interaction with Bill and the others was one of those rare moments of seeing the real William Shatner.

Another time I was due to meet Bill on the set of *Star Trek V: The Final Frontier*. I arrived during the shooting of a scene in which Kirk and Spock were to speak with Scotty and then run down the tunnel to exit left. It took 26 takes to get the scene; each time they tried it something would happen to ruin the scene. Finally, it looked good and Bill and Leonard came running off camera. Bill was hopping up and down in front of Leonard who stood stoically quiet, hands clasped behind his back — a typical Spockian pose — while Bill danced in front of him feigning punching Leonard in the stomach while chorusing "We got it, we got it!"

Finally, looking down into the eyes of his excited friend, Leonard simply shook his head side to side very slowly. "No?" muttered Bill, mimicking the head motion. Leonard just nodded, and shook his head again. Bill finally shrugged his shoulders in capitulation and turned on his heels for yet another take. I remember thinking, 'They really are Kirk and Spock; they just don't know it.' In any event, they finally managed to put the scene in the can but it was not easy and I marveled at how they kept up the energy and freshness necessary for the same shot, scene after scene.

Somewhere between the 15th and 25th take, we got the interview pinned down but it was another one of those "God help me" interviews. They turned the lights out so I couldn't read my notes, plus we had to whisper so my tape recorder only picked up every fourth or fifth word. Interviewing Bill Shatner was often challenging.

Take the time I had to follow him around on the grass while he was getting ready for a workout with his trainer. Bill wanted to hold the recorder so he could dictate some of the material. Satisfied, he finally handed it back to me and we concluded the interview. When I looked down at the recorder I realized that the machine was in the "off" position. The tape was blank. Bill felt terrible and offered to redo the interview but his trainer was waiting. I told him not to worry, that I could manage just fine. As soon as he disappeared around the corner, I sank down on the grass and wrote furiously, praying fervently, *Please Lord let me remember.* I managed to get something down but I sure couldn't swear as to the accuracy of my writing, not that day. Fortunately, Bill never complained so I guess I was close enough — or he was kind enough not to say anything.

Shatner with FEDCON host and moderator, Marc B. Lee. (Photo courtesy Marc B. Lee)

If the interviews were a bit of a risk, the Weekends were the ultimate challenge, but they were also my most favorite time with both Bill and the fans. I really looked forward to it every year. Besides being a great time for everyone to get to know each other, we also used the Weekend as our main fundraiser for the club's number one charity, the Hollywood Charity Horse Show. Club members came from all over the world to attend, as well as from all over the United States, which made it even more exciting.

When announcing the Weekend we always published a

statement to the effect that should a business commitment conflict with the Weekend, then, obviously, the business commitment would take priority and the Weekend would be canceled. In 1995, the impossible happened and for the only time in 20 years we had to cancel the Weekend. We had three weeks before the due date and immediately notified the attendees of the cancellation. Everyone was very understanding. The problem was, two members from Germany, one from Australia, and one from Maine who we were not able to contact in time arrived in L.A. several days before the Weekend was due to start. They were devastated when advised that we had been forced to cancel. I contacted Bill's office and explained the situation and asked if he could possibly spare any time to see them, it would mean so much to them. A few hours later I got a call from Bill's assistant who said that if I could arrange to bring the members over to his office the following morning, Bill would see them.

Promptly at 9 a.m. the following morning, I brought four astounded ladies in to meet with Bill Shatner. He spent almost an hour talking to them, sharing jokes and generally making everyone feel special. He then signed one of his books for each of us and arranged with the *Star Trek* office for a special tour of the *Next Generation* set, which, incidentally, was closed to everyone except us. Brent Spiner pretended to speak German to them and Jonathan Frakes joked about how pathetic his speaking was. The fans felt that no Weekend could possibly have compared to that day.

One of the great privileges of running the fan club was that I got to videotape the conventions, and the tapes were then sold for charity. Most of the time there was no problem but on the 25th anniversary there had been some serious death threats against both the actors and the convention directors. The result was a tightening of security and a shutdown of the usually amicable attitude you find at conventions. When it came to the taping I was advised the answer was absolutely NO. This was a closed house, meaning you had to be a member of the union or you couldn't videotape anything. I tried to explain to the house manager that we were just a fan club and the videos were used for charity. I was not a member of the union but could I join for just the night? Was $26 enough since that was all I had? He looked pretty threatening as he grabbed hold of a chair and told me to sit down on it and stay still. He left me sitting on a chair in the middle of this huge stage with people busily running all around me, shouting all kinds of orders, but I was too scared to move. What seemed like hours later (but was probably only about 30 minutes) he came over to me and signaled for me to follow him. Dutifully, I did, hauling my camera with me. We went out front of the stage, down the stairs into the pit where I was introduced to the *Entertainment Tonight* crew and was told I was now the newest member of the team. The crew members were all in on the deal and were so great helping me to set up for the best possible spot for my filming of the show. My camera was so small compared to theirs! My only real problem was I didn't have my tripod so I spent an hour and a half filming while trying to keep the camera steady aiming up at the stage. I would have given anything for someone to help hold up my arms, but it didn't happen. They just hurt while I kept filming. In any event I got some great material and we made good money for the disabled children the Horse Show supports every year.

William Shatner and Bill Campbell (Squire Trelain) raising money for charity at a Shatner Weekend, 1995. (Photo courtesy Joyce Mason)

The Hollywood Charity Horse Show was the club's favorite charity. Bill had started it back in 1990 when he saw some kids doing spectacular things on the back of a Clydesdale. That may not seem like much but these kids were part of a physical therapy group called Ahead With Horses and most of the kids were unable to walk when off the horse. One was blind and another was missing both her arms. Bill lost his heart to them that afternoon and as the last child dismounted Bill vaulted over the wall and ran into the center of the ring. With tears running down his cheeks he decided then and there that he would do something to help these kids. Thus was born the Hollywood Charity Horse Show. It is still going strong and plays every

April to help three children's charities, and the fan club, happily, is still an integral part of the Show.

One of our members who came to every Horse Show was Micki Paller. Micki was very quiet, rather shy, incredibly loyal, and dedicated to her job of taking tickets every year. She would travel from her home in the Midwest to L.A. every year to stand quietly at her gate taking tickets all evening, never asking for time off or complaining that it was too cold, too boring, or that she was unappreciated. So we decided to present Micki with a Certificate of Appreciation from the William Shatner Connection and Bill would present it to her. I never got around to mentioning to Bill that we were planning this because I knew he would have no problem with it. That evening at the banquet, I read the Certificate citing Micki's loyalty and much to everyone's surprise, mine included, Bill yelled out "That's Micki!" and headed straight for her. The look on Micki's face was one of incredulity. She simply could not believe that Bill actually knew who she was. We took pictures of her with Bill making the presentation and later sent them to her after having them autographed. That weekend was like a miracle to Micki, to one who never expected anything, nor sought any thanks. Micki died three months later in her sleep. She was a beautiful soul whom everyone loved. Her brother explained it was a heart attack and she probably never felt anything. He also wrote me to say that he used to feel concern that his sister led too solitary a life and he worried that she really didn't have a life, until after her death when he received letters from all over the world expressing how much they would miss Micki, how loved she was. He had no idea how happy she was but he would never again criticize her fan club. He understood now how rich her life really was.

In the final analysis, the existence of a fan club like the William Shatner Connection may not seem all that important. Then again, in this world of terrorism and war, maybe we need the fantasy of heroes. Perhaps if we can appreciate our heroes, even make-believe ones, by banding together on our Web sites and through our newsletters and shared experiences, maybe it will help someone to smile, and feel better. If it helps to dry a tear or two, then that is a very good thing.

What a Con!

Some people just watch the shows from the safety of their living rooms, but you can't call yourself a real, diehard fan unless you've been to a *Star Trek* convention. The conventions run year-round, everywhere in the world, and are either put on by Creation Entertainment or the fans themselves. The cons raise money for charities, offer fans merchandise they might never see anywhere else (from T-shirts to props used on the show), and give people a chance to meet the celebrities face to face (if you pay the right price) or listen to them speak to the group. Official conventions can be very costly, and occasionally aren't worth the big bucks charged at the door, but generally they are a fun weekend where online friends meet in person for the first time, spend lots of money, and come away satisfied.

"Is This a Proposal?"

BY MIKE WITT

A.K.A. CAPTAIN EKIM

In the old days, starting back in the '50s, I used to watch television shows like *Buck Rogers, Flash Gordon, Lassie, Lost in Space, Star Trek*, and *Battlestar Galactica*. As with most people, I gave little thought to ever meeting any of those people I saw on the screen. There were no sci-fi conventions for those of us who watched the likes of *Flash Gordon* or *Buck Rogers* (the original *Buck Rogers*, I mean) back in the '50s or early '60s (I think I just dated myself). Nor were there any sci-fi fan clubs that one could join to share this interest (at least, none that I was aware of).

But by the late '60s and early '70s everything was all starting to change. A group on the East Coast decided to organize a convention for *Star Trek* fans and, lo and behold, *Star Trek* conventions were born; so was Creation Entertainment. There were also sci-fi organizations forming such as Star Fleet International (SFI), International Federation of Trekkers (IFT), United Federation of Planets (UFP), followed by an assortment of Klingon and Romulan clubs and other *Star Trek* organizations, including the United Federation of Planets Internationale (UFPI).

In joining one of these organizations through a local chapter, I discovered that I was able to share my interest in *Star Trek*/sci-fi with people who not only lived in my area, but in other parts of the country. I am able to communicate with them on a listserve and when on a trip, it is not unusual to be invited to stay with them.

The thing I really like about *Star Trek* is the camaraderie that it creates. The sharing of an interest with others who have the same interest, be it at a convention or at a chapter meeting. Because of my interest in science fiction in general and *Star Trek* in particular, I have had that chance. At the time of this writing, I am the CO (or President) of a UFPI chapter in San Diego, CA. The chapter name is Com Station Z and because our chapter started out as a computer BBS, we became a communication station, as opposed to a vessel, as most *Star Trek* chapters are.

There have been times when Com Station Z members have driven several hundreds of miles to "play" with another chapter. We have gone to Las Vegas to ride the "*Experience*" together and attend the "Klingon Feast" there, and gone to "Mouse Trek" at Disneyland. But along with the playing, we also contribute to our communities by volunteering at such events as the Foster Family Association Picnic, San Diego Parks and Recreation Disabled Services Holiday Program, the Hollywood Charity Horse Show (L.A. Equestrian Center), Ahead With Horses (Sun Valley, CA), and Crime Stoppers 5k walk/run fundraiser. We also volunteer at Creation conventions in Los Angeles, San Diego, Las Vegas, and Phoenix.

I have been volunteering as a crowd and autograph line control person at Creation Entertainment conventions for over five years, and as such, I have met a lot of those actors whom I used to watch on TV or in the movies during my younger days. Some of these actors, who are really just people like you and me, have now become friends of mine. I have also met people from all over the world who attend the larger Creation Grand Slam conventions in Pasadena. The funny thing is that after a while, as you volunteer, you run into the same people at different conventions who, at the very least, become acquaintances.

For the most part, volunteers usually meet or are near the celebrities who attend these conventions. Some get to sit next to the celebrity and feed him or her pictures from those attending the convention to autograph, or escort them around the convention or to their car. Believe it or not, one sometimes has to escort the celebrity to the bathroom.

I have several stories about celebrities. At Grand Slam 2000, I was invited to dinner with BarBara Luna, Celeste Yarnall, and Grace Lee Whitney (who played Yeoman Janice Rand in *ST: TOS*). I didn't go because I was still at "work" volunteering and I did not know Grace that well at that time. Believe me, I heard from some of the other volunteers later that when a celebrity asks you to join them for dinner, you go. Forget the volunteering, just go. I later got a chance to talk to Grace as we did have something in common. Grace is a 20-year recovering alcoholic. I don't think that she will mind my saying that, because she speaks about that subject at conventions. My wife of over 26 years also had a drinking problem, and it killed her. So, because of this common link, Grace and I sat and talked and I got to know her. She is a very, very nice lady!

I ran into Grace again at a Creation Entertainment convention in Las Vegas in January 2001. It was over two hours before the convention opened and I went over to say hello. We got talking about alcoholism programs and the people. Before we knew it, it was time for the convention to open. It was at about that time that she said that what she needed in her life was a person who understood alcoholics, alcoholism, and the programs. To which I replied, "Is this a proposal? It sounds like you are asking me to marry you." So, for the rest of the two-day convention, Grace and I were "engaged." Even actor Jeff Rector

Mike "Ekim" Witt and Grace Lee Whitney at a convention in Las Vegas, January 2001. (Photo courtesy Mike Witt)

got into the act by giving me a wedding brochure from the hotel chapel. He suggested that I ask her what ceremony package she wanted. Grace and I took it all in stride and had fun with it all weekend.

My next encounter with Grace was at Creation's Grand Slam 2001 in Pasadena. I threw a surprise birthday party for her at the convention, as her birthday fell on one of the con days. So I got a cake and a card and we all sang "Happy Birthday" to her.

Another time I told Garrett Wang to go park in a public lot across the street from the Pasadena Center. It was one of those times when my job assignment was to secure the top of the driveway that leads to the underground parking at the Pasadena Center. I had a list of who was to arrive that day and Mr. Wang was not on it. So, when he drove up, I didn't recognize him at first. It wasn't until after I told him to park across the street that I finally figured out who he was. I did let him go down the drive to park, after which he walked back up to talk to two of his friends who had arrived at the top of the driveway and I got my picture taken with him. He said he was going to tell everyone what I told him to do when he got on stage. Whether he did or not, I do not know, I never got into the auditorium that day to hear him.

So, *Star Trek* has affected my life in a most positive way. I feel very fortunate to be in the position I am in at this time. I now have an extended family of fellow Trekkers to associate with and I can count some of the actors from the programs and movies among my friends. There are even vendors who have become friends of mine after seeing them at convention after convention. Most of all, I have a family in the members of our chapter. There is a whole family of Trekkers out there, all trying to live the dream of the Great Bird of the Galaxy and IDIC and I am part of it.

Meeting the Great Bird

BY JONATHAN LANE

It was January of 1984, and while most of George Orwell's predictions for that year hadn't come true, the world was still a very interesting place. For *Star Trek* fans, we were eagerly wondering if Spock would come back from the dead in the upcoming third *Star Trek* movie. We were years from an *Enterprise* with an "A" and even further from a "D".

Star Trek conventions were still a relatively rare thing. In fact, Creation Conventions was still just a small science-fiction store located in Mineola, New York, and they would put on only a few *Star Trek* conventions each year in a very limited number of cities. These days, Creation Entertainment is synonymous with numerous grand, sweeping conventions covering all genres of science fiction. If you've ever been to any of the recent Creation cons (which are now more regimented and controlled), you probably won't believe the following story ever happened. But it did — cross my heart.

I was 17 years old and attending my first *Star Trek* convention in New York City at the Roosevelt Hotel near Grand Central Station. The major *Star Trek* guests were Walter Koenig and Gene and Majel Barrett Roddenberry. In those days, having Gene and Majel at a con was a special treat because Gene would always bring his special black-and-white, uncut copy of the original pilot episode, "The Cage." Videotapes were only just beginning to become commonplace, and most fans had only ever seen the "chopped up" version of "The Cage" that appears in flashbacks during the two-part episode "The Menagerie." Today, most fans have seen the uncut version of the first pilot, but back then, you only saw it when Gene Roddenberry came to a con.

Having just finished wandering around the dealers' room early Saturday afternoon, I was still in "explore" mode, experiencing as I was my first-ever con. There wasn't too much to explore, though. Aside from the dealers' room, ballroom, and a smaller room filled with free stuff and fan club tables, there wasn't really anything to see.

Except for this one small room off to the side of the freebie room . . .

I hadn't noticed it before because the door had been shut. It was a small conference room with a table and about 20 chairs. Most of the chairs were filled with convention-goers, and everyone seemed to be listening to someone at the front of the room. I wandered in and took a seat towards the back.

It was Gene Roddenberry!

He was chatting with the fans, telling stories and jokes, giving his opinions on a wide variety of topics. Apparently, he had been wandering around, killing time until his scheduled talk in the ballroom, and some fans had started talking to him. Eventually, enough of a group had gathered for Gene to suggest going into this small conference room to sit down and continue the conversation. They left the door open for anyone to come by and join in. (Today, something like this would never happen at a Creation convention!)

While I don't remember all the things Gene talked about, I do have two very lasting impressions. First, he was one of the warmest, sincerely enthusiastic people I have ever seen. He loved being there and chatting with the fans. And my second impression was that Gene couldn't stay on a subject for more than about a minute before going off on a tangent, and then another tangent, and then another. He was just so enthusiastic about so many things, and quite knowledgeable, too. And all these thoughts just wanted to burst out of his mouth all at once. I remember feeling frustrated every time Gene would go off on a tangent because the story he'd been telling was so interesting. But then the next story would be even more interesting. Then he'd get sidetracked again. But it didn't matter.

This was the creator of *Star Trek*, and I'd been given a rare opportunity to sit down and chat with this amazing man.

About 45 minutes later, it was time for Gene to go on stage. A Creation organizer came in to get him, and he said he'd be right there. In trying to finish up, Gene started yet another tangent. It took two more visits by the frazzled Creation person before Gene was finally able to pull himself away from this small conference room and go on stage.

Years later, I heard stories and read biographies that said Gene was a real hard-ass, tough to work with and stubborn as an ox. Other reminiscences describe him as welcoming and friendly. I'll never know which was the true Gene Roddenberry, and maybe he was all of those things. But on that winter day in New York City, he was just a big kid talking to other big kids about anything and everything . . . and loving every minute of it.

Who's Michael?

BY CHRISTINA LAKE

It was time to line up for Tuvok's autograph. I was with my family at Toronto Trek IX, a popular *Star Trek* convention, in 1995. As is common at most cons, each paid guest was permitted one free autograph per star and my eldest daughter, Natalie, asked me to help locate a picture of Tim Russ for him to sign. We scanned all the booths, and asked the dealers if they had any pictures of him left and the answer time and again was, "Sorry, no." We were getting desperate.

We started to check the booths outside the dealers' room

and, in an out of the way spot, came across a small table staffed by a good-looking young black man. Displayed for sale were copies of an artist's rendition of Tim Russ as Tuvok. The man greeted us and asked my daughter if she was going to get Tim Russ's autograph. She said, "Yes." He looked around and, seeing no one nearby, handed a copy to Natalie.

He said, "These cost $5, but you can have one for free. Just tell Tim that Michael said, 'Hello.'"

I looked him in the eye and said, "Who's Michael?"

"His brother," the man replied, his eyes sparkling with mischief. We smiled back in delight and he quickly put his finger to his lips. "Shh, don't tell anyone here." We nodded and thanked him several times.

After waiting in the huge lineup with a thousand other fans, we arrived at the signing table. A thrilled Natalie got Tim's autograph, the signature of the artist, and a few words of encouragement. Many years later, Natalie is enrolled in high school where she is taking enriched art and architecture classes. She wants to be an artist some day by going into animation, architecture, or graphic design. Wherever you are, Michael, thanks again.

Birthday Wishes from Captain Janeway

BY DAVID JOHN BENISTON

Captain Janeway is my one and only role model. I think she is absolutely amazing and it's always her best episodes of *Voyager* I watch when I'm feeling down or depressed (because I used to get bullied quite a lot).

Kate Mulgrew waves to fans at the FEDCON 6 convention. (Photo courtesy Susanne Dörfler)

So, for my 18th birthday, I thought it would be prudent to do something that I could look back on and be proud of as a Trekker. So I decided to go to my first-ever convention!

My ticket number was quite late, so I thought I'd never get the one and only autograph I wanted from the convention. But I did, I met Kate Mulgrew. I know she won't even remember me, but I said my piece: "I'd just like to say Kate, it's my 18th birthday today. And I'm honored to have met you!" to which she replied, "Oh happy birthday!" I'll never forget the tone she used, so kind and genuine! I'll treasure that moment for the rest of my life.

History Repeats Itself

BY GERALD GURIAN

I can honestly declare that I do not remember a time when I was not a passionate fan of *Star Trek*. As *The Original Series* celebrated its 35th anniversary during 2001, I witnessed my 40th. Indeed, growing up on reruns of the adventures of Kirk and crew, I feel comfortable in stating that *Star Trek* played a pivotal role in shaping and influencing my fundamental moral character and basic understanding of right and wrong. For aside from providing superb and exciting action entertainment — with a healthy dose of exotic and scantily-clad women thrown in for good measure — *Star Trek* provided a bona fide cast of larger-than-life heroes espousing core values such as honesty, integrity, loyalty, bravery, compassion, self-sacrifice, and perseverance despite seemingly insurmountable obstacles.

While other television series of the times were caught up in ethnic stereotypes, *Star Trek* presented a bold vision of a multinational, multiracial crew operating in harmony and bound by their common thread of humanity. By the 24th century, we were assured that Earth would have solved the devastating problems of mass poverty, hunger, and disease, and mankind would no longer be divided by petty politics or racial prejudice.

Perhaps this overwhelmingly positive portrait of humanity

overcoming hardships and peacefully exploring the galaxy is another major factor in the global appeal of the *Star Trek* franchise. Of course, as a teenager who was caught up in the action-adventure and beautiful women on the show, I doubt that I fully appreciated the subtle influences or underlying social commentaries that were being made at the time.

At the age of 14, when I took pride in my abilities to associate specific stardates and planets with particular events in the 79 original series episodes, and could readily describe all of the intricacies of starship operations and technology at a minute level of detail, I had my first exposure to a unique *Star Trek*-inspired phenomena: the convention.

The year was 1976 and a *Star Trek* convention was being held for the first time in my very own hometown of Toronto! From July 23 to 25, the event was taking place in a number of ballrooms and conference rooms at the Royal York Hotel downtown, and in addition to a number of episode writers and space experts, no less than six of the *Star Trek* television stars were to be on-hand: James Doohan, George Takei, Nichelle Nichols, Walter Koening, Grace Lee Whitney, and Mark Lenard.

Needless to say, I found that the event was able to live up to all expectations: one conference room was perpetually screening all original series episodes in Super 8 format; there was a huge life-size mock-up of the *Enterprise* bridge on display in another ballroom; and intriguing panel discussions on NASA space, and science fiction were being held. I recall a huge dealers' room where every imaginable kind of *Trek* merchandise item was on sale, fans were competing against one another in an extravagant costume show and, of course, the *Star Trek* stars were regularly appearing on stage a couple of times each day to

Nichelle Nichols receives flowers from adoring fans. (Photo courtesy Susanne Dörfler)

provide behind-the-scenes insights, share humorous stories, and take audience questions.

The most exciting aspect of the convention, though, was the opportunity to personally meet and get autographs of the stars at special signing sessions. It was at one of these that a particularly memorable event took place for me. I must admit that, along with probably the entire male population of North America, I had developed a crush on Nichelle Nichols, who played Lt. Uhura. I still believe that she ranks as one of the most beautiful women ever to grace our television sets in the history of that media. All of the *Star Trek* stars went out of their way to put the fans at ease and were very gracious with their time, even pausing to chat with each fan a bit after signing for them. The same was also true of Ms. Nichols. And despite being awestruck in her presence, I somehow overcame my youthful shyness and asked Nichelle if I might give her a kiss. She smiled, and I recall her bringing her face close to mine and then allowing me to place an innocent kiss on her cheek. After that momentous event, I was truly in heaven for days!

Surprisingly, the story of that kiss does not end in July 1976. Seventeen years later, in the summer of 1993, I found myself living and working as an engineer in the Grand Rapids, Michigan area. I had graduated in the mid-'80s from the University of Toronto with a degree in Industrial Engineering, and after working for five years in Canada I had decided to boldly go and pursue a life south of the border. As I reviewed my convention mementos to write this passage, I realize the full coincidence of the situation: the dates on which this next large *Star Trek* convention took place were July 24 to 25, almost exactly the same dates as the previous one. The DreamWerks convention was being held in Chicago, just a few hours' drive from Grand Rapids, and again six *Trek* original series stars — almost exactly the same lineup as before — were to be present: James Doohan, Nichelle Nichols, George Takei, Walter Koenig, Grace Lee Whitney, and Bruce Hyde. In Chicago, I joined the autograph line that had formed for Nichelle Nichols with no underlying desire other than to relate to her the circumstances of our meeting 17 years earlier and to thank her for a past kindness. I had actually brought along a large white plastic bag emblazoned with a Toronto *Star Trek* '76 logo to prove it.

After relating the story of the kiss to Nichelle, I was very surprised when she rose from her chair at the signing table, and stated, "History should repeat itself." On this occasion, the kiss was directly on her lips and just as pleasant as the first time. What was different, however, was the spontaneous applause that immediately followed the second kiss, as the large crowd in the autograph line that had witnessed the event began to cheer loudly. I am certain that not too many fans can claim to have kissed the lovely Nichelle Nichols ever, much less on more than one occasion, and certainly not to such cheering.

That 1993 Chicago convention provided another memorable opportunity to interact and spend time with a great *Star Trek* star: James Doohan. After a special late evening on-stage appearance that featured a unique photo opportunity with individual fans, Mr. Doohan surprised those of us who had remained past the official end of the event by accompanying us to a table in the hotel ballroom and chatting informally for almost an hour! I was seated right across from James along with about four others at the table; and perhaps another five or six fans were standing to either side. Mr. Doohan allowed a fan to buy him a drink and talked freely about his career and solicited our thoughts and questions.

I told him of our shared Canadian roots; and he reminisced about his early radio days with the CBC in Canada. When I mentioned that I had been inspired in my choice of profession by *Star Trek* and his role as Chief Engineer, he related that a great number of engineers had confided in him that they were similarly influenced by "Scotty," and it was clear that Mr. Doohan took great pride in that. Indeed, I can recall that the premiere of a new *Star Trek* motion picture was treated as a major social event in my university engineering community. Mr. Doohan also proudly mentioned that he was the recipient of an honorary engineering degree himself!

I can assure my fellow fans that when one question was raised about his impressions of William Shatner, the rumor that there is little affection felt for his former colleague is certainly true. I felt it unfortunate that there was still ill feeling after so many decades; Bill Shatner has indicated in his own autobiography that he wasn't sufficiently sensitive to his co-actors' desires for on-screen dialogue when he made his own suggestions to modify the *Star Trek* shooting scripts. Mr. Doohan said he had a great admiration for Captain Kirk, but not for Mr. Shatner. One other interesting revelation from the discussion was that none of the original series cast members actually saw any significant financial rewards from the tremendous success that the show experienced in network syndication. As no one could have predicted the phenomenal success of *Star Trek*, the cast had just signed standard television contracts that provided for the payment of royalties only through the first few reruns of each episode. However, Mr. Doohan did imply that the oversight was addressed when it came time to negotiate the motion picture contracts.

It was on August 16, 1997, in Novi, Michigan at the age of 35 that I finally came face to face with William Shatner, and the experience could not have been more exhilarating and obstacle-ridden. For a number of years I had virtually given up the hope of ever meeting Mr. Shatner in-person; his convention appearances had become quite rare, and his typical visit consisted solely of an on-stage presentation, with immediate transportation to the airport following his concluding remarks. Thus, there was almost no opportunity for personal interaction with fans, and certainly no prearranged autograph sessions. In the late '90s, however, William Shatner abruptly changed his long-standing practices and began dramatically increasing his visibility at conventions. Furthermore, he would often consent to sign autographs for the first 300 fans in some cities who purchased "Gold Circle" tickets through the convention sponsor. For a $100 fee, I could realize a life long ambition of meeting the man who had inspired me so tremendously with his portrayal of the Captain of the *Enterprise*!

As I recall, I submitted my order for the convention ticket approximately three months before the event itself was to take place. I was intent on obtaining a Polaroid photo of myself with Mr. Shatner, which would prove to be the cause of some tense moments on the afternoon of the 16th. I remember that Mr. Shatner gave a fine speech to the audience, with a particularly enjoyable anecdote about hiding Leonard Nimoy's bicycle in the rafters of the soundstage as a practical joke. As I had attended the convention alone, I would have to enlist the assistance of my fellow Gold Circle ticket-holders to take my highly coveted Polaroid. It was in this task that the fates seemed to have conspired against me! My fellow fans were more than willing to offer their assistance, but on three successive attempts I waited for the Polaroid to develop only to discover that the photography had been horribly mishandled. One photographer had inadvertently blocked part of the flash mechanism and the picture was shrouded in darkness; a different fan had moved the camera while releasing the shutter and I saw a tremendously blurred image; and another would-be assistant took the shot prematurely while I was walking up to pose with Mr. Shatner

The coveted Polaroid — fourth time's a charm! (Photo courtesy Gerald Gurian)

and only part of my arm was visible in the photo. After each successive failure, I told Mr. Shatner of the misfortune that had occurred, and he graciously invited me to pose again with him for another attempt. The fourth try met with resounding success, and I finally had in my possession the perfect photograph. I was greatly impressed with the uncalled-for level of kindness that William Shatner demonstrated in enabling me to obtain my photograph, and I am quick to relate this story to anyone I meet who derides his perceived treatment of fans!

George Takei is without a doubt one of the most popular of the Star Trek *stars. I've included two stories about him in this chapter, and this first one is written by the current FEDCON (in Bonn, Germany) host and moderator:*

My Friend George

BY MARC B. LEE

My first entry into the *Star Trek* scene was in early 1987. Ten years earlier, I had seen *Star Wars* the day it opened and then 11 times in one month after that.

So I like science fiction. So I dream of space flight and aliens and ray guns and computer generated imagery. Does that classify me as a freak? As some sort of weirdo who still lives with his mother, has a pocket protector, and wears his pants a few inches closer to the chest than most? Hell, no! I was different. I looked normal, acted normal, and have kissed a girl once or twice in my life. So let me tell you what I found out about the people who happen to love *Star Trek* and why they like going to those things called conventions.

Watching *Trek* on TV in my youth was a sheer fascination to me. It was one of many hobbies I had and shared with baseball, model building, comic books, and girls, not necessarily in that order. I wasn't sure what a Trekkie was, but I knew what a bookworm was. I never associated the two.

Starlog magazine had advertised the 20th anniversary convention to be held in Boston, Massachusetts, and I knew I was going to be there. I didn't know what a *Star Trek* convention was, but I knew there would be some big names there: Gene

Roddenberry, Majel Barrett Roddenberry, George Takei, Walter Koenig, and Robin Curtis. Wow! I'm going! I'm there! I'm excited! I'm broke! *I'm broke?*

Once I dug up the cash, I flew out the door, caught the first flight, and ended up at the hotel where the action would take place.

George Takei was my first *Trek* buddy. I became George's assistant at the con in Boston and it came about in a very strange way. I arrived at the hotel early the day before things were to get underway. I didn't have anything to do so I thought I'd hang out in the lobby of the hotel. I took a book with me to keep me occupied and it was a *Star Trek* novel. I had never read one before but thought I would look "cool" if I ran into someone who was there for the convention and they saw me with a *Star Trek* book. This was the first sign that you've become a fan — having something *Star Trek*-related in your possession for everyone to see.

While I was "hanging out," one of the staff members for the convention noticed me (the book worked) and asked if I was there for the convention. I told him that this was my first and asked if he needed any help in setting up. He said yes and I spent the rest of the afternoon getting to know other staff members and the layout of a convention gathering. While I was fascinated, I was a little confused at the complexity involved in hosting such an event. I wondered if this was what people had to go through to do a con and my knowledge about such things increased through the years to come.

The staff liked me and asked if I would be a chaperone for Mr. George Takei. I said "Sure!" They explained to me what the job was and I searched feverishly to ask one simple

George Takei gathers his fans for a morning jog, with Marc acting as his bodyguard. (Photo courtesy Marc B. Lee)

question: "That sounds great, but . . . who's George Takei?"

Ahem.

Who could forget the helmsman, swashbuckling, soon to become Captain of his own ship character known as Sulu? Well, I guess . . . me. Names and faces are not my forte.

In the course of my assignment to George, I had learned

that he was a fellow who appreciated the fans in a different way than the *Trek* celebs I later worked with. George genuinely loved to listen to his fans. Not that the others didn't, but George asked associative questions of the stories the fans relayed to him. He enjoyed the eclectic lives these people shared with him and showed his gratitude in return. Whereas some celebrities, in my experience, hurried to complete their paid responsibilities, George remained with his fans long after the dinner bell had rung. He not only continued to share a bit of his experiences and personal life while off stage, but he allowed us to rekindle our acquaintances when we had met again. George was someone I truly respect. (I still wanted to kill him for those damn early morning group jogs around unfamiliar terrain in strange cities [see page 149] but I respected him nonetheless.)

Once I had escorted George around that convention, I had learned that I was the one who needed protection, not George. During those early years of *Trek* cons, fans were seeing their star up close for the first time. When I wasn't hustling George to point B from point A, the fans saw a hole in my down time and decided to belly up to me for more info on that favorite star of theirs. Thank goodness George had my back. He had that infectious laugh and subtle naiveté that soothed the masses. He knew when to accommodate. I'll never forget him for that. My friend George.

I thought maybe to stir things up a bit I'd put in a story by someone who hasn't always had positive convention experiences.

An Open Letter to Con Participants

BY BRIAN LOMBARD

I've noticed that every time a *Trek* convention comes to Washington, D.C., some sort of national tragedy takes place a few days earlier. In the summer of 1998, a gunman stormed the Capitol building and murdered two police officers. That weekend, I went to Novacon, a now defunct convention that used to hold two shows every year. One of the guests at that convention was Marc Alaimo, a.k.a. Gul Dukat from *Deep Space Nine*. Alaimo started off his stage appearance by talking about the shooting, and he kept with it for much of his stage time. Those of us who were there in the audience felt that it had really changed the tone of the whole show. It was depressing, and that's not why we go to conventions.

In April of 1999, two teenagers in Littleton, Colorado, went on a murderous rampage at Columbine High School. That weekend, I went to another Novacon, and the special guest was René Auberjonois, who of course is known to *Trek* fans as Odo. *Deep Space Nine* had wrapped production of its final episode, "What You Leave Behind," the day before. Auberjonois had gone straight from the wrap party to the airport, and flew all night so he could be at our con the next morning. But rather than saying much about the end of *DS9*, he wanted to talk about Columbine. We certainly didn't want to seem heartless, but by that point, it had been the only thing anyone had been talking about for four days. The convention was supposed to be a break from all that, but again, this feeling of dread came over us as we realized it was Alaimo all over again. I haven't been to a convention since.

It's now kind of an old joke among my friends and me. We see an ad for a convention, and we say, "Uh-oh, what's going to happen this week?" We watch these shows and attend the cons as a form of escapism. We know what goes on in the real world, and that's why so many of us like *Star Trek*, because of its positive look at the future. It takes us away from the often bleak and depressing events that bombard our newscasts every night. I can understand that the actors need to talk about these things, but I don't think that they should dwell on them. If you have to, ask the audience for a respectable moment of silence, and then move on. Cheer us up. Tell us about *Trek*.

Those Pesky Cameras

BY KEVIN BARRETT

I wanted to share a story that shows the generosity and decency of James Doohan. I attended a convention in Boston where Doohan was the main guest. He gave his talk (in various accents), and then invited fans to ask him questions. He wandered around the audience, holding his mike up to each questioner, letting fans get their picture taken with him, and just being generally friendly. I came up with some question regarding the "Relics" episode of *TNG*, but it was really just a lame excuse to have my cousin (who happened to be there) take my picture with James Doohan. James was very gracious and patient and smiled broadly for the picture.

When I got back to my seat, I learned that the camera had malfunctioned and there was no picture. Later during the convention, James was very busily signing autographs and obviously a bit on the weary side. When I got an autograph and explained what had happened with the picture, he immediately suggested that I come around the table and get the picture taken again. I did, and it came out great! I was so touched that he was such a nice guy.

Nothing makes a place feel more like home than people who enjoy the same things as you do; especially when you know more about it than they do . . .

Klingons Are the Same Wherever You Go

BY STEVE COHEN

I have always been a huge *Star Trek* fan. About five years ago I was visiting England on business, doing research for a chemical company for about a week and a half. It was probably the longest, most boring business trip I had ever been on. (Bradford, England is not the most exciting place on Earth.) Anyway, I was due to leave the following day, and I couldn't wait.

Friday evening I got back to my hotel room around 5 p.m. I took a shower, got dressed, and was going to walk around town, get something to eat, and maybe catch a movie. I get out of the elevator in the lobby and couldn't believe my eyes. There were Klingons in the lobby! I was in shock. It turns out that there was a *Star Trek* convention happening in this boring town the entire weekend. As I walked around the lobby I felt like I was at Starfleet Headquarters. Everyone was dressed in either a Starfleet

"Klingon" Jeff Nichols poses with Walter Koenig, George Takei, and James Doohan. (Photos courtesy Jeff Nichols)

uniform or an alien costume. There were viewing rooms to watch episodes and dealers selling anything imaginable.

I ended up hanging out drinking with a group of Klingons that evening, and I had such a great time I didn't want to leave. I stayed up the whole night drinking and watching episodes. The broadcasting of *DS9* was behind that in the U.S.; the fans had only seen up to season two or three and I had already seen season five or the beginning of six. So, at the request of a huge group of them I answered questions and told stories about the coming episodes all night. It was a great time and an experience I will never forget.

If you've ever been in an autograph lineup, you know one of the most annoying things is someone who completely hogs the actor's time, especially when the volunteers are pushing you through the area like cattle.

Who Cares If She's Greek Orthodox?!

BY BRIAN LOMBARD

Meeting a *Trek* actor at conventions is always a highlight, but often, some fans let their interest in a star preclude common courtesy. In 1994, I attended a convention in Washington, D.C. Marina Sirtis, who was playing Counselor Troi on *TNG* at the time, was one of the invited guests. Her stage performance was great. She had us all thoroughly entertained. *The Next Generation* was coming to a close, and Marina was giving us some end of the series insight.

After her speech, my friends and I headed over to the auto-

The lovely Marina Sirtis at FEDCON 8.
(Photo courtesy Susanne Dörfler)

graph line, which was already pretty considerable by that point. By the time we got to the front, we had been standing for about two hours. We didn't mind the wait, because at least we were going to meet her and "have a moment" with the actress.

The person in front of me went up and got her signature, then left. It was finally my turn. I walked up to Marina and handed her a photo. We barely got out our hellos, when the gentleman came running back, and said, "Miss Sirtis, I forgot to ask. Are you Greek Orthodox?"

I felt sorry for Marina, because it was obvious she was ticked off, but she continued her discussion with the fan. He finally walked off, and she handed me the photo back. That was it. I was done. He had robbed me of "my moment." I don't know who he is. I don't know where he is. But to this day, I can't think of that story without wanting to beat the guy.

Data in Drag

BY MIKE HATHAWAY

Back the in early '90s, there was a convention called TexTrek, held in Arlington, Texas. Majel Barrett Roddenberry was one of the guests. At the time, I was part of a comedy troupe, *Star Trek: The Fan Generation*, performing as Data in live 30 to 45 minute spoofs of *ST:TNG*.

In a last-minute decision, I cobbled together some bad Data make-up, threw together some Renaissance court wear and took Data further back in time than shown in "Time's Arrow Pt. 1," improvising my way through five minutes of "Data in the Renaissance" for the costume contest. Much to my surprise, I won the "Best of *Trek*" category.

Majel herself was one of the award presenters. After she hung the medal around my neck, she reached down to my crotch, grabbed my over-stuffed codpiece and asked "So what's this for?" I was shocked!

Another convention, a couple of years later, the comedy troupe had dissolved, but I now had a solo act, "Data in Drag," once again based on a Western episode, this time being the end of "A Fistful of Datas." After an appearance at Conniption in Dallas, Texas, I was still in full make-up and dress and hanging out in the hotel's sports bar, where the Saturday night dance was being held. I walked up to the bar to get a drink, right next to two of the bar's regular patrons, obviously hanging around to watch the "freak show" in progress around them.

One of the rednecks was eyeing me up and down in the dim golden light of the bar and said to the bartender, "Get the lady whatever she wants."

I smiled politely, looked the bartender straight in the eye and said in my deepest voice, "Bourbon and Coke." I took my drink, tipped my glass to my stunned patron and slinked back to my friends' table. The look of sheer horror on that redneck's face is something I'll cherish as long as I live.

Keep on Trekking

BY GAIL DOOD

My interest in *Star Trek* began in 1991 while spending a month in a hospital waiting for emergency repeat surgery on an aneurysm in my brain. My surgeon was on vacation, and rather than try an unknown doctor I waited for his return. My husband and friends were wonderful, but at the end of visiting hours another long night stretched ahead of me. It was hard to sleep not knowing if I would awake the next morning — the aneurysm could blow at any time.

One night, during my usual channel-surfing, I came across *Star Trek: The Next Generation.* I left it on mostly out of curiosity, but I found the events unraveling before me so uplifting and full of hope for the future of mankind that I sought out the program every night. The result was that I felt better when the lights went out, and I was able to go to sleep at peace with the world.

My surgeon eventually returned, and my skull was opened

once more. This time, however, lots of things went wrong and during the surgery I had a stroke. The prognosis was bad but I beat the odds once more, and in a few months I was back in the game again.

I continued to watch *ST:TNG* throughout my recovery as I fought hard to be whole again. I heard about Brent Spiner being at a convention near where I live in Arlington, Virginia, and asked my husband to take me so that I might see my favorite *Trek* star. We went on a Sunday afternoon and I found a seat in the large ballroom. Unfortunately, I was too far away from the stage to see Brent well, but his presentation was wonderful. Seeing the Trekkers in costumes and talking with other fans, I knew I, too, was a Trekker. Since that day I have been attending more and more conventions. Even though my family sometimes wonders about me, I keep on trekking.

Majel Barrett-Roddenberry on stage at a FEDCON convention. (Photo courtesy Marc B. Lee)

Going to the same cons every year I have made lots of new friends. In 1994, at a Shore Leave convention in Maryland, someone told me about DS495, a fan club near where I live. I looked into it, liked what I saw, and joined. The club needed a treasurer and my background was in accounting, so I volunteered. In DS495 I enjoy the companionship of a diversified group of friends. I've even learned new skills: parking cars at a charity baseball game, handing out food and water at charity races in downtown Washington, D.C., dressing like a mutant and scaring people in a haunted house, and answering phones for Jerry's Kids. I love this club because whenever we're needed, we show up and do our best.

For a few years I "dressed" for the cons and won trophies for my Lwaxana Troi presentation, thanks to a fellow DS495er who made the dresses and put me together. It was great fun being the glorious Mrs. Troi for a few hours. I haven't done her for a few years now, but she may show up again. I eventually met Majel Barrett-Roddenberry and showed her the photos of my costumes. Of all the *Trek* stars, I've found Majel to be the most accessible. She whole-heartedly approved of my impersonation of her and urged me to carry on. Meeting the First Lady of *Star Trek* is a memory I'll always remember.

Meeting General Martok

BY JACQUELINE BUNDY

My story is not about myself, but about an experience my two young sons had that just thrilled them to bits. We are a multi-generational family of fans, and whenever possible my children attend conventions with me. It is always a lot of fun to share the experience with your children.

In the summer of 2000 my two sons, Andrew and Adam, then ages eight and nine, attended their first convention, the Fantasticon in Los Angeles. One of their biggest heroes is J.G. Hertzler, who plays Martok on *Deep Space Nine.*

After seeing Mr. Hertzler on stage they were thrilled to discover that they could actually meet and talk with him afterwards in the autograph room. He was extremely kind to them, patiently answering their questions, teasing them a bit in a kind, good-natured way. Before we left he insisted on giving them autographed pictures and graciously posed for some pictures with them. The boys were in heaven and talked of nothing else for weeks.

In March 2001 the boys attended the Grand Slam Convention in Pasadena with me. They had been inspired by seeing fans in costume at the Fantasticon and had asked me to help them make Klingon costumes. We spent a lot of time on the project and they drew a lot of attention dressed as *TOS*-style Klingons.

Once again they patiently waited to see their hero Martok. Imagine their delight when Mr. Hertzler remembered them from the previous year and complimented them on their costumes! They were thrilled. But the best was yet to come for Andrew and Adam.

Later in the day we were taking a break outside and the boys were playing near the entrance to the convention center with their Klingon toys. J.G. came out and when he saw them he stopped to talk with them and fool around a bit. A photographer from the StarTrek.com site was there and took the boys' picture with J.G., which was posted on the StarTrek.com site in the fan photo section.

Andrew and Adam were so excited, and said to me, "We're famous and everyone knows that Martok is our friend!" It was an experience they'll never forget.

George Takei Gets Arrested for Jogging

BY JONATHAN LANE

When my friend Jack Eaton first told me the following story, I wasn't sure if it was true or not. But then, a few years later, I asked George Takei at a con and discovered that, yes, Mr. Sulu was once arrested for jogging! Read on . . .

It all started many years ago in Boston when Jack Eaton went to pick up George Takei and David Gerrold (who wrote "The Trouble with Tribbles") at the airport. Jack was one of the convention organizers for the Boston *Star Trek* Association (BSTA) and both George and David were scheduled to appear. Through a series of mishaps involving two sets of luggage, Jack was forced to leave his van unattended in a "No Parking" zone. With George and David and their bags finally collected, Jack returned to his van just in time to see it being towed away. Running and jumping in front of the tow truck, Jack was somehow able to talk them into unhitching it, therefore avoiding disaster . . . or at least a major cab fare back to the convention hotel.

Later on, after George and David were settled in, the fan club organizers held a little mixer in the hotel lounge. Each one of the convention organizers had a name tag with a nickname on it. Jack's said "Crocodile Eaton," (the movie *Crocodile*

Dundee had recently been released and was popular at the time). George took a look at this name tag and said, "Oh my, no! That will never do." People looked back at George in puzzlement. George continued, "Your name isn't 'Crocodile.' Oh, definitely not. It's 'Tow Away'!" Everyone laughed (except Jack), and the name stuck. Even years later, Jack was known as "Tow Away" Eaton.

The "Tow Away" incident led to a series of practical jokes exchanged between Jack and George. At the following convention, while on stage, Jack presented George with a pair of boxer shorts with the words "Don't call me 'tiny'!" written across the front. George later retaliated in good fun, and so it went for a few years . . . until Jack delivered the final, decisive prank.

It occurred at another BSTA convention, this time in Bangor, Maine, where Jack just happened to have a friend who worked in the Bangor Police Department. Coincidentally, it was also the weekend of George's birthday.

George Takei is seriously committed to staying healthy and physically fit, and he tries to get others to take care of themselves as well. He goes jogging every morning (or at least he did), and during convention weekends, he'll often invite fans to come along jogging with him. I myself once joined him on my bike — and I still couldn't keep up with him!

Knowing that George was scheduled to go jogging at 7 a.m., Jack had some friends knock on his hotel door shortly after 6 a.m. He opened it, "Yes?"

"Mr. Takei? Are you still planning to go jogging?"

"Yes. Why do you ask?"

Looking a little concerned, they answered, "Because there are a bunch of people waiting in the lobby to go jogging with you, and they were wondering if you'd already left or if you weren't planning on going at all."

"Oh," George thought for a second, "Tell them I'll be right down. I just have to get dressed."

A few minutes later, George got to the lobby to discover no one was there waiting for him. One of the people who had knocked on his door told him, "They thought you'd already left, so they went to catch up with you. They headed off in that direction."

George looked outside, "I'll see if I can catch up with them," and started jogging in the same direction.

It should be noted, at this point, that there was no jogging group that had already left. It was necessary for the prank that George be jogging alone, and by getting him out of the hotel at 6:15 a.m., the other *Star Trek* fan joggers wouldn't be there yet.

And so George had his morning jog, and at about 8 a.m. he returned to the street where the hotel was located. As he crossed at the light, a police car pulled up next to him. The officer asked him to stop and then proceeded to get out of the squad car.

"Sir," the cop began, "Were you jogging over on Maple Street about a half hour ago?"

George looked confused, "I might have been. I was jogging, but I don't live here, so I don't know the street names."

"Sir, are you aware that you were jogging in a 'No Jogging' zone?"

"A what?!"

"We have a city ordinance, sir," the officer explained, "To avoid traffic congestion and accidents, certain areas have been designated as 'No Jogging' zones."

George was dumbfounded.

"I'm going to have to write you up a ticket, sir."

"For jogging? That's ridiculous!"

"We received a phoned-in complaint, sir. I have no choice," the cop began writing in his ticket book.

George started yelling, "But I didn't know! I live in Los Angeles! You can't expect someone who's not from here to know about something so preposterous!"

"There are signs posted, sir," the officer kept writing.

"I didn't see any!"

"They're posted, sir. It's not my fault if you didn't see them."

George was fuming. "This is the stupidest thing I've ever heard! I thought we had crazy laws in L.A., but this one takes the cake! You should figure out a better way of letting visitors know about this idiotic rule!" Meanwhile, a crowd of fans was gathering in front of the hotel, wondering what was going on.

The officer was still writing, "Name?"

"What?"

"Can I have your name, sir?"

"George Takei. T-A-K-E-I." George added in a hopeful voice, "I play Sulu on *Star Trek*."

The cop wasn't impressed. "Date of birth, sir?"

"Today, actually. Today is my birthday."

Again, the cop wasn't impressed. He finished writing the ticket and pulled it out of his book, handing it to George. "Sir, I need you to read over the information on the front of the ticket to verify that it's correct. Then I need you to read the back and let me know if you have any questions."

George took the ticket in disgust. He looked at the front and then turned it over. Handwritten on the back was the following note: "Happy Birthday, George. GOTCHA!" Signed, "Tow Away."

George started laughing so hard he almost fell over.

Yep, the cop was Jack's friend, participating in the prank while off-duty. It wasn't a real ticket book either. According to Jack, a video camera was set up in the lobby focused on George and the cop, and on the front seat of the squad car was a tape recorder. Apparently, there is a video somewhere of this entire "incident."

So George Takei wasn't exactly arrested for jogging, nor was he really even ticketed. But in the practical joke "competition" between our Mr. Sulu and the resourceful "Tow Away" Eaton, I think "Tow Away" was the clear winner.

These last two didn't actually happen at a convention, they happened at Star Trek: The Experience *at the Las Vegas Hilton. The exhibit is a $70 million collaboration between Paramount and the Hilton, and I received several stories about visits to it (see "More Than Just Fans" for another story). These two were my favorites because they showed the actors employed at the Hilton actually know their stuff!*

Don't Try to Argue with a Ferengi . . .

BY KEVIN WAGNER

My wife and I took a vacation to Las Vegas and visited *Star Trek: The Experience* at the Las Vegas Hilton.

There was a shopping area that resembled The Promenade from *Deep Space Nine* and was filled with *Star Trek*-themed stores, including Garak's Clothier and Moogie's Trading Post. The shops are filled with *Star Trek* memorabilia ranging from an inexpensive

T-shirt to items priced in the thousands. Need a place to get a fitted Klingon Battle Suit? It's yours for $12,000. The clerk assured me that two had already been sold. Kahless would be proud.

I was browsing a possible purchase of a tricorder replica when a very realistic Ferengi asked me if I was going to buy that. When I shook my head, the Ferengi exclaimed, "What good are you?" He was disturbed at how hard it was to make a profit.

I was so startled I couldn't respond, and the Ferengi moved on when he was solicited with photo requests, which he was happy to oblige. Recovering, I asked if he was charging. "No," he answered.

Ah ha! I had him. "Anything worth doing is worth doing for money," I pointed out. I wasn't Ferengi, but I did know the Thirteenth Rule of Acquisition. But he was unfazed.

"Don't quote the Rules of Acquisition to me, Hu-Man. Free publicity!" he replied sharply. I didn't have a chance to respond before another customer appeared and yelled, "Quark!" with glee. The Ferengi sighed. "Billions of Ferengi in the Universe and they all think we are Quark." I could only nod in agreement. (On the other hand, he did look a lot like Quark.)

I left with a positive experience. If I have one regret, it's that it's not close enough for me to go back. I've finally thought of a comeback for that Ferengi.

. . . Or a Klingon

BY MARK "IRVING" SMITH

As a big fan who has seen every episode of each *Star Trek* series, it's fair to say that a lot of the vocabulary that might not otherwise infiltrate my ways of phrasing things, does. It was plainly clear while at the *Star Trek: The Experience* in Las Vegas. There we were, walking through the museum leading up to the ride, when the line started backing up. Usually, that's not supposed to happen, since you're supposed to walk past people who are standing still, checking out the exhibits. So as we rounded the corner, I decided to bellow out, "So you're the P'tok that's been holding up the line!"

Now I'm not sure whether I was consciously aware that three mean-looking Klingons were the ones I had decided to insult, but the result was having to endure five minutes of ridicule for being a scrawny human with a "primitive laser device," which was actually a laser I built into a Type II Phaser keychain.

Later, they spotted me at Quark's and decided to torment me some more by insulting my choice of the "Phaser Fire" smoothie. I guess the "Warp Core Breach" would have been a better choice. A little while after lunch, I was browsing The Promenade. When I asked one of the wandering Klingons (he was probably drunk from too much blood wine) if it was a "good day to buy," he almost drew his disruptor for contaminating their ways with Ferengi ideals . . .

Oh well, at least they offered me a job in engineering on their Bird of Prey when I finished college. There's something to aspire to!

A Friend in Need . . .

It's amazing how a television show can transcend its role as pure entertainment, and can instead spark discussions that lead to friendships, and sometimes even more serious relationships. Sci-fi television shows and movies have always provided an escapist fantasy world that attracts people who are happy, people who are lonely, and people just looking for a change from their daily routines. But when that show also has a fanbase of people with similar feelings, it can bring people together. The following stories are about fans who found friendship, love, and even closer family ties through *Star Trek*.

From Heartbreak to "Root Beer"

BY ANDY MIHAIL

I've always been a *Star Trek* fan, mostly since I saw *Star Trek 2: The Wrath of Khan* on the big screen, but the real change in my life came when I got divorced at 24 years old. That devastating event happened in April 1994. Later that year in November, *Generations* was released, and I went alone to see it. There in the lobby, a *Trek* fan club was holding a party to help promote the film.

Right away, some of the members noticed me. Not for what I was wearing (a *Trek* shirt like other fans), but because I had written a story on their small convention for a local news station where I was working at the time. I had gone on my own time on a Saturday afternoon with a camera and gathered video and interviews (again, a post-divorce activity) and put it all together in a neat little package for Monday's newscast. The fan club members were very grateful and told me that they received a positive response from it. They made me feel at home, and for the first time in months, I felt like I mattered again. Needless to say, I joined the club that night.

The organization, I found out, was worldwide. Calling itself "The International Federation of Trekkers," each of its chapters is encouraged to do whatever they can to help the community around them. I jumped right in and quickly became one of the core members of that chapter, traveling and doing whatever they needed me to do. With this group, I've been to a dozen conventions, and seen and met everyone from William Shatner to Armin Shimerman, from Jimmy Doohan to Robert Picardo, from Robert O'Reilly to Michael Dorn. But my favorite was meeting Terry Farrell! In my book, she's a 10. I was rather star struck when I was doing security at the stage, and promptly melted when she gave me a hug and kiss on the cheek after I got my photograph taken with her. It's an 8 x 10 on my wall right now. Needless to say, I got teased for months afterwards from the other members.

The chapter I was in (in northwest Indiana) held small con-

The Founding Four, clockwise from top right: Andy Mihail, Betty Fay, Wendy Mihail, and Kimberly Fay. (Photo courtesy Andy Mihail)

ventions that benefited several local groups. The conventions raised money for children with cancer, and helped the local college's athletic scholarship fund that was short of money that year. We never had any "big name" stars, but we sure had some great guests — Patrick Stewart's stand-in, Dennis Tracy, and *Next Generation* extra Tracee Lee Coco. Both were fabulous and had great stories to tell.

Well, somewhere in this melee, I met my present wife (v2.0, as I like to say!) who liked *Trek* also. Soon, both of us were interchangeable. You asked one to do something, and you got an extra set of hands as a bonus. It was such a joke in the chapter that they started calling us "root beer"; my name is Andy, hers is Wendy . . . A&W (yeah, we groaned, too).

Eventually we moved to Massachusetts and decided that we had so much fun in that chapter, we wanted to start one here. It started off with just four members a little over two years ago, and has grown to 12. We are just starting an ongoing recycling drive to help out a local animal shelter, one of many things we've accomplished in our short tenure. One of the crewmembers is now one of my best friends and the godfather to my beautiful daughter, Samantha.

I've also gotten two more hats to wear in the IFT organization. I'm now a chapter commander to the *U.S.S. Corona*; the GEO 4 Commander, which means that I'm in charge of all the chapters in New England and New York; and I'm on the Council Prime as the Director of Communications. It's a position where I make sure the members know what the Council is doing to help out the organization as a whole.

So *Star Trek* has definitely had a major influence on my life, and it all started because Gene Roddenberry once told IFT founder Russ Haslage that he'd like a club that does what the *Enterprise* does: ". . . to go places and help people."

Death of the Great Bird of the Galaxy

BY DAN FOSTER

Back in 1991 I was fresh out of high school and was always surrounded by my Trekker friends. We had all been fans since before *The Next Generation* appeared, but gathered every Monday night at my apartment (much to my young wife Jennifer's chagrin) to watch Picard and the gang boldly go where no one has gone before. One night we decided to play "Star Trek: The Role Playing Game," and give my wife a break.

We went over to Andie and Andre's house, leaving Jennifer to herself. Paul, Grady, Bill — we were all there, and had a great role-playing session. I was the game master, it was an original series campaign, and we just gave everyone the classic characters because Andie and Andre were new to role-playing. It was rousing, full of every *Trek* cliché there was: time travel, starship battles, saving the world.

When it was over we all went home. Everyone was happy after the great adventure we'd had. I walked in, and my wife looked at me strangely. I asked her what was wrong, and she said to me, almost apologetically, "Gene Roddenberry died today."

I was crushed. I'd never met the man, and I never suffered from the illusion that Roddenberry was a saint, but he had given the world an adventure that we could all not only enjoy, but learn from. He held up a mirror that showed us not what we were, but what we could be.

I called my friends that night, and we all agreed that we would miss him, but even without knowing it we had celebrated him that night by sharing in the human adventure he had left for us. Could he have appreciated anything more?

The Internet has opened up so much for sci-fi fans. More than ever before we can connect with other fans from around the world, learn new insights and inside scoops on the shows, and find new ways of expressing ourselves:

SimTrek

BY HEATHER BARON

I've never actually met a star or even been to a convention, and I don't know much about the *Star Trek* universe. But, I am involved in a *Star Trek* role-playing game that has changed my life.

Exactly one year ago I was surfing the Web for things to do. I was interested in *Star Trek* and had become obsessed with *Voyager*. I stumbled upon a site and noticed that it was a game online where you would take the role of a character and "sim." In other words, act out a plotline.

So I downloaded the program that would allow me to get to the place where they would sim (mIRC) and entered the main channel in which to chat with the members. From that point on my life changed. I have friends from all over the world. I met my best friend there. I helped a friend out of his depression. I have a second mom. I have touched so many people's lives and have had my life changed in return. I had always been shy and this place has opened me up, allowed me to experience different cultures and learn things that I wouldn't have known otherwise.

Our simulations pretty much run into each other. When a major part of one story ends, another one starts up, just as it would in real life. My characters and the characters of others in my organization are real to us. They do probable things that any real person would do; they are just based in the *Star Trek*

Alice Krige, a.k.a. "The Borg Queen," answers questions at a fan convention. (Photo courtesy Susanne Dörfler)

world. In the plot that we just finished, for example, powerful ships came from another universe and destroyed the Federation and all other ruling powers of the alpha quadrant. The FFO's Flag Ship — the *U.S.S. Peace Keeper* — had to travel back through time to fight off what we called the "derelict ships" and save the Federation's future. That plotline was what we called a fleet sim. It impacted every character and each player in the organization and whether they were in group simulations or just simulations with one or two people they were impacted and revolved around the main plot.

After spending one year in this group that had been founded many years ago, I have become a high-ranking official. I hold a position on the Command Staff, the heart of the organization. And I am a role model for other simmers. Known simply as The Cute Bajoran, or Cecil by the people there, I have been able to make something of my life. Instead of sitting in front of the tube for 12 hours a day, I am interacting with others, making friends, and helping people. The things this organization has done for me are incredible, and I will always hold the people there close to my heart.

Finding Love Where You Least Expect It

BY DAVID DEAKIN

In 1989, my mother pointed out a small article in our local paper, the *Herne Bay Times*, about a young woman from a nearby town who was setting up a *Star Trek* fan club for people in our county. I got in touch, attended some of the early, informal meetings and took on the job of producing the club newsletter.

Twelve years later that young woman is my wife, Grace. We're no longer involved in running the club, though "Treknet Kent," as it is called, still exists.

Star Trek was a common interest that brought us together, a foundation on which we built a lasting love and friendship. We still love and watch *Trek* (we saw the pilot of *Enterprise* for the first time last night), but like so many other fans we found much more in each other than the media will have you think Trekkies are capable of.

A Toast

BY SCOTT WRIGHT

My friend David and I caught the *Star Trek* bug in 1972 when the show first started running in syndication in Oakland. We were both nine years old, and spent a lot of time acting out our own adventures of Kirk and Spock. We collected the books about the series — *The Making of Star Trek, The World of Star Trek, The Trouble with Tribbles* — as well as the novelizations by James Blish. We even tape recorded the shows, which led to some disagreements with my mother, who was annoyed when I wouldn't allow the dishwasher to run between 6 p.m. and 7 p.m.

On August 7th and 8th in 1976, *Space: The Final Frontier #2*, was held at the Oakland Auditorium. David and I attended, wearing our Starfleet uniform shirts that we had bought (after saving up several months of allowance) at the Federation Trading Post in Berkeley. The convention was like a huge playground to a couple of 13-year-old boys who could already quote a lot of the dialogue from a variety of episodes. The Master of Ceremonies was Bob Wilkins, a self-professed fan of the show and host of *Creature Features*, which ran on the same network as *Star Trek*. We saw the blooper reel, watched episodes on the big screen, spent time in the dealers' room, and sat in on Q&A's with William Shatner, Leonard Nimoy, DeForest Kelly, and Arlene Martell (T'Pring from "Amok Time") among others. My dad (who drove us to the con) even took a picture of us at a park nearby with me giving David the "Vulcan Neck Pinch."

During our high school and college years, David and I did not see as much of each other, but we'd get together periodically and kept in touch by telephone. When I got married in 1985, David was

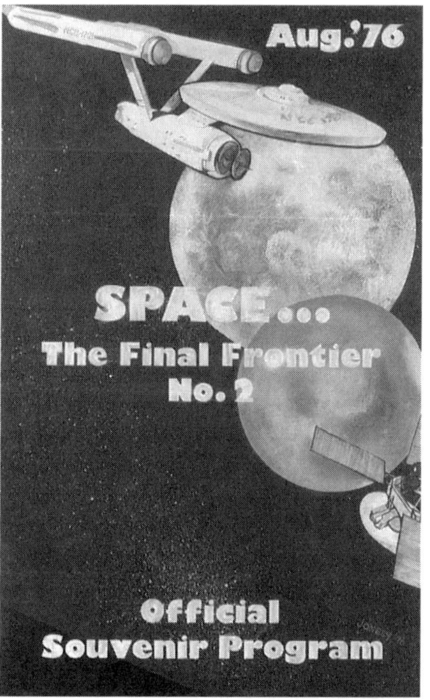

(Above) David winces as Scott applies the Vulcan Neck Pinch. (Photo courtesy Scott Wright)

(Right) The program from the 1976 convention. (Courtesy Scott Wright)

my Best Man. During his toast, David related a variety of things about our friendship over the years and how he and Dianna (my wife) became friends, but he finished it off by describing those two days at that convention in '76, saying it was still one of his most cherished memories. Many of the guests were not privy to just how special that was or the significance it still held.

Not long after, David came over to my house and I told him I had something to show him. To his amazement I produced that photograph of the two of us at the park (which he made me swear I would never show to anyone) and the program from the convention. "Yeah," I said, "those two days still mean a lot to me as well."

In 1995, David got married and I was his Best Man. He still lives in Northern California and works as a computer technician in San Francisco. I moved to Southern California about three years ago and am pursuing a career in acting as well as being an IT tech for a brokerage firm. We're separated by distance, but stay in touch to this day. I still have the program from *Space: The Final Frontier #2* and the photograph from that very special weekend in 1976.

Brothers in Trek

BY DAN HARRIS

I've been a *Star Trek* fan for a long time, and have seen every episode of every series. However, I don't dress as a Starfleet Officer or study the Klingon language. I just enjoy watching the show. I am very grateful to *Star Trek*; besides being a great series, it is because of the show that I met my closest friend.

It was the end of the summer of 1986 and I had started college a couple of weeks earlier. One day I was a little bored, so I went downstairs to the second floor of the dormitory (I lived on the third) to walk around. I noticed a room that was wall-to-wall *Star Trek* posters, and I stood in the doorway gaping. No one was in the room. Someone walking by asked me what I was doing there, and I told him that I was admiring the posters. The person walked into the next room and said, "Henry, someone here wants to see you," and Henry came out.

Henry was a year ahead of me in college. We had no classes in common. Although we had similar political beliefs, he was not active in any student groups. We were both active religiously, but our religions were very different (I'm Jewish, he's Roman Catholic). If not for the *Star Trek* posters, Henry and I probably never would have met.

Within a week Henry and I were best friends. It's been 15 years since, and three more *Star Trek* series and six more movies have come and gone. We have lived together three times since that meeting. I never had a biological brother, but I consider Henry to be one; neither of us is afraid to tell the other that we love him.

Henry is a very kind and good person. He is understanding of others and compassionate. I was once very angry with another friend, so I asked Henry how to get back at him for what he did. Henry responded, "You could always forgive him." The other friend and I are still friends to this day. My wife said that I described Henry almost as being larger than life. However, after spending some time with him, she found that he lives up to my description.

When Henry got his Ph.D., his mother threw a big party for him. I was asked to make the toast, and I chose to paraphrase a line from a *Star Trek* movie: "Of all the souls I have encountered, his is the most humane." Everyone at the party knew I spoke the truth.

I am very grateful to *Star Trek*, for if not for *Star Trek*, I would never have met my "brother" Henry.

Finding Friendship on the Aurore

BY MARCO DI LALLA

Star Trek. Who would've thought those two simple words could change my life? I remember so clearly the first time I answered NO to a friend who insisted on showing me what kind of incredible series *Star Trek: The Next Generation* was. Big mistake! Not long after, I finally agreed to sit in front of that old television set and watch an entire episode ("Descent") without taking my eyes off the screen. Little did I know, I had just reached a turning point in my life.

I became so addicted to the world of *Star Trek* that within two months, I had watched every single *TOS* and *TNG* episode, plus all of the movies (six at the time). Since then, I have started a collection of *Star Trek* books, posters, games, cards, uniforms, etc. I've even made it a personal mission to understand exactly how a warp drive works. In detail.

I literally embrace the ideas and visions of Gene Roddenberry. Not a single day goes by without me wondering if, eventually, humanity will conquer all of its problems and difficulties, just like it's been accomplished on *Star Trek*. Gene's vision of how humans could be in 300 years has affected me so much that I tend to think of *Star Trek* as actually being the real fate reserved for our species.

To my surprise, I found a similar way to express what *Star Trek* means to me. One day I was surfing the Web when I came upon a French *Trek* site. The creators of that Internet Web page were inviting me to be part of a *Star Trek* role-playing game. I had never been interested in that type of game before. "And through the Internet?" I thought to myself. What kind of role-play is that? But what the heck, I filled out the submission form and soon after, there I was, receiving the first e-mail that would ignite a passion.

The game is called "*Star Trek* Québec," and it enables you to create your own character along with his or her background story, and then puts that creation on board a fictional starship, where you get to coexist with other members of the club.

I had never felt so appreciated before. For the past couple of years, I've had the opportunity to write great stories and share them with other people across the world. In turn, they would continue to develop my idea until it finally reached completion, thus writing an entire story based on the *Star Trek* universe. On that fictional ship, called the Aurore, I've spent nights

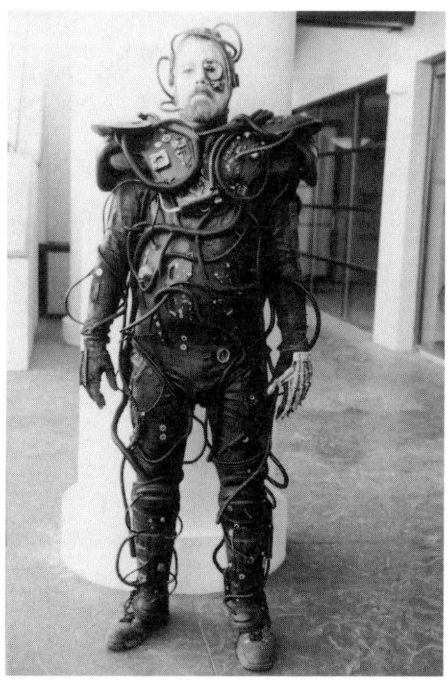

"The Borg do not discriminate; we just assimilate." Fan Mark Stempfly dresses as Borg Drone 6 of 9. (Photo courtesy Mark Stempfly)

coming up with a good plotline that would send our little crew on yet another bold mission!

There are 14 ships similar to mine, for a total of 300 to 400 members. This brings me to the relationships I've created with so many of them. Every once in a while, activities are organized where as many members as possible get to meet face to face. During such events, I've had the pleasure of discovering for the first time in my life that I could talk freely and openly about the *Star Trek* phenomenon without being teased, laughed at, or called a freak.

I have made some great relationships with certain people from the club. I now consider them the best friends I ever had. Just like me, they truly hope Gene's vision will one day come true. With them, I have shared a passion and a dream. They have literally become a second family to me, and over time we've learned that we have more in common than *Star Trek*. Together, we traveled to a convention in Toronto, where we got to meet Jonathan Frakes, Roxann Dawson, and J.G. Hertzler. I even got to shake hands with Eugene Roddenberry, Gene's only son!

Whenever life gets rough, I try to think of a *Star Trek* episode in which the crew of the *Enterprise* or *Defiant* or *Voyager* figures a way out of a situation that seemed impossible. That's what *Star Trek* has brought to me: confidence, strength, and imagination. Combined with my newfound friends, I can honestly say that no other TV show could ever bring as much satisfaction.

This was a very touching story that many people can relate to: not fitting in while at school and finding friendship with other Trekkers.

Fitting In

BY MARK BIRD

As I was growing up, my family moved around a lot both here and abroad, so I had no specific focus in my life that I could use as an anchor. I was also miserable because wearing glasses made me a target of the usual stereotypes at school. It wasn't until I turned on the TV one Wednesday night at 6 p.m. that I had found something that I enjoyed: *Star Trek: The Next Generation*.

Leonard Nimoy salutes the audience at a fan convention. (Photo courtesy Susanne Dörfler)

The episode was "Pen Pals," and I felt that it captured my feelings at the time perfectly: a lone voice crying out into the void, desperate for someone to listen to it. Then, out of the darkness, comes the sound of a single voice crying back: this plotline summed up how I felt and what I needed so badly. I had friends, but at the time they were few and far between. When I found *Star Trek* I discovered there were many people who watched it and enjoyed it as much as I did.

From there, I went in search of others, specifically at conventions and fan clubs, who had had the same experience. I went to a fan club meeting and was immediately welcomed. I finally felt like I belonged somewhere — here was a place where I could talk openly to people without fear of ridicule.

This group has followed me in my life from then on. I am now 17 years old and remain friends with everyone in the group. I have become a lot more confident and am happier as a consequence.

Star Trek has also taught me that, in the future, there is the chance that humankind will evolve to the point where differences can be overcome and where society can rebuild itself, working collectively to advance beyond the constraints of this world and expand to others.

Of all of the stories I received from fans for this book, none touched me the way this one did. This is a very powerful story about life, death, and hope, and shows that Star Trek *sometimes has such a far-reaching impact, it can help us through times of our deepest sorrows (and not only stretches across the uni-*

verse, but into the afterlife). If you've ever doubted the show's power, this story will make you a believer.

A Cry from the Soul

BY AVRIL STORM BOURBON

A.K.A. K'LANNAGH O'SULLIVAN, HOUSE OF E'TOH

I have been a *Trek* fan since childhood, and a fan of Klingons in particular, both the original and current style. My favorite character of all time is K'Ehleyr, Worf's half-human, half-Klingon mate. She is the inspiration for the persona that I assume for cons; K'Lannagh O'Sullivan, half-Klingon, half-Irish human. I'm a professional costumer, and have always loved to "play dress-up," so roaming about as K'Lannagh is a great joy and release for me, as I get to be loud and boisterous and fierce and friendly, which I am normally . . . but somehow, when you've got that crest on your head, people don't seem to mind!

I have known and loved many friends I've met at conventions who also play Klingon, but the most Klingon of them all was my friend and "Captain," Chuck. The man lived, breathed, and ate Klingdom; he knew *every* word to *every* Klingon song ever sung on *Trek* (much to the surprise of "Martok," J.G. Hertzler, when Chuck sang for him!), and was totally devoted to Klingon fandom. Sadly, he was killed in a car accident in February '98, in a fierce El Niño rainstorm. His mother and family were devastated, but they knew how much Chuck loved his Klingon friends, and we were very welcome at his funeral (no, we didn't wear our costumes, but several of us did wear our Sashes of Honor over our mourning clothes). Chuck's wonderful mom allowed us to stay at the end of the service, until most had left. Then we explained to those who remained (Chuck's mom had been fully involved, and gave her consent ahead of time) that we were his Klingon friends, and that being a Klingon was very important to him, and that to honor him as a Klingon we would now gather around him and send him out with a Klingon Death Howl. We explained that it would be loud, and it may be disturbing to them, but it was what he wanted.

Of all the times in my life that I have grieved for someone, this experience will be the one I will actually remember fondly, and with joy. We gathered around his coffin, said goodbye, and then took a deep breath. It started out as a hum, low and deep. Then a cry, a howl, deep from the soul. A cleansing scream that said both "Why?" and "Goodbye, friend" ripped from my throat, such as I wanted to let in the past when a loved one had passed, but never felt the freedom to do so. To our surprise, several of his family members joined in towards the end; clearly, they felt the same freedom to let out, full throttle, the sorrow they'd been feeling for nearly a week.

When our breaths were spent, our shoulders sagged with relief, like a weight had been lifted. We would always miss him, and remember him, but with joy. We had sent him to Sto-Vo-Kor, and warned the dead of his arrival, as he would've wanted. We embraced each other, reveling in our friendship, knowing all too well now that life is short, and to never take that nearness for granted.

We walked outside, where it had been raining all day, when suddenly, a *huge* bolt of lightning arched over our heads, and a loud clap of thunder boomed, vibrating through me. We jumped, and then laughed ourselves to tears.

We knew it wasn't a coincidence. It was Chuck, saying goodbye and thank you.

He'd made it to Sto-Vo-Kor, where the blood wine flowed freely, and all the Honored Dead were singing his story.

When people make fun of Trekkers, especially those of us who run around cons dressed as Klingons, and call us geeks and nerds, I shrug it off. Because I know better. Everyone needs something to believe in, to carry on. Everyone needs somewhere to belong. If being a Klingon makes us "weird," so what? I'm proud to belong to a group of wonderful, loyal, creative people. I am proud to live my life with honor.

I am proud to be a Klingon! tlhIngan maH!

Attention Trekkers and Trekkies!

Do you have a story to tell that could have been in this book? It could be featured in a future volume of *Trekkers: Stories by Fans for Fans*. Have you met one of the cast members? Has your life changed because of the show? Tell us about it. You can reach us at ecwpress.com, and e-mail your stories to jen@ecwpress.com. Or mail your story to us at:

ECW Press
2120 Queen Street East, Suite 200
Toronto, ON
M4E 1E2
Canada

We'll get back to you and let you know if your story will be featured in a future book!